Microservices Design Patterns
for Serverless Applications

Design, Deploy, and Dominate the Agile Development Landscape.
Your Practical Guide to Building Agile Beasts!

Katie Millie

Microservices Design Patterns for Serverless Applications

Design, Deploy, and Dominate the Agile Development Landscape. Your Practical Guide to Building Agile Beasts!

By

Katie Millie

Copyright notice

Copyright © 2024 Katie Millie - All Rights Reserved.

This work is the exclusive intellectual property of Katie Millie. All aspects of its content, including but not limited to the written text, images, graphics, and design elements, are comprehensively protected by international copyright laws. Unauthorized use, replication, or distribution of any portion of this material, whether in whole or in part, without the express written permission of Katie Millie, is strictly prohibited and may result in legal action.

Katie Millie retains all moral rights to this creation, ensuring her right to be acknowledged as the author and to prevent any use that could harm the integrity or reputation of the work. These rights safeguard her ability to object to any modifications, distortions, or other derogatory treatments of the material.

We deeply appreciate your respect for the intellectual property rights of the author, as such consideration plays a crucial role in sustaining and nurturing ongoing creative endeavors. Your cooperation is invaluable in protecting the originality and integrity of this work. Thank you for your understanding and support.

Table of Contents

INTRODUCTION

Chapter 1

    The Agile Dream: Building Applications with Speed and Flexibility

        The Microservices Revolution: Breaking Down the Monolith

            The Serverless Game Changer: Unleashing Microservices from Infrastructure Woes

                Why Serverless and Microservices? A Perfect Match for Agile Development

Chapter 2

    Core Concepts of Microservices: A Service-Oriented Approach

        Benefits of Microservices: Agility, Scalability, and Maintainability

            Challenges of Microservices: Communication, Complexity, and Testing

                Designing Effective Microservices: Best Practices and Considerations

Chapter 3

    Introduction to Serverless Computing: A Pay-as-You-Go Revolution

        Benefits of Serverless: Focus on Functionality, Automatic Scaling, and Cost Efficiency

            How Does Serverless Work? Events, Triggers, and Functions in Action

                Key Features of Serverless Platforms (e.g., AWS Lambda, Azure Functions)

Chapter 4
  Choosing the Right Programming Languages for Serverless Functions
    Serverless Frameworks: Simplifying Development and Deployment (e.g., Serverless Framework, AWS SAM)
      Integrating with APIs and Data Sources: Building the Microservices Ecosystem
        Monitoring and Debugging Tools for Serverless Applications (e.g., AWS CloudWatch)

Chapter 5
  What is the API Gateway Pattern? Centralized Management and Security
    Benefits of API Gateway: Streamlining Access and Simplifying Development
      Implementing the API Gateway Pattern with Serverless Technologies
        Best Practices for Designing Effective APIs for Microservices

Chapter 6
  Understanding Event-Driven Architecture: Microservices Reacting to Events
    Benefits of Event-Driven Architecture: Scalability, Loose Coupling, and Flexibility
      Implementing Event-Driven Microservices with Serverless and Event Queues (e.g., SQS)
        Real-World Examples of Event-Driven Microservices (e.g., Order Processing)

Chapter 7

The Challenge of Long-Running Tasks: Blocking Microservices and Performance Issues

The Async Processing Pattern Explained: Offloading Work for Efficient Microservices

Implementing Async Processing with Serverless and Work Queues (e.g., SQS, Lambda)

Best Practices for Designing Microservices for Asynchronous Work

Chapter 8

Understanding Fault Tolerance: Protecting Your Application from Failures

The Circuit Breaker Pattern Explained: Detecting and Handling Errors Gracefully

Implementing the Circuit Breaker Pattern with Serverless and Monitoring Tools

Ensuring Fault Tolerance and High Availability in Your Microservices Architecture

Chapter 9

Securing Your Microservices: Authentication, Authorization, and Encryption

IAM Policies and Roles for Serverless Functions: Granting Least Privilege

API Gateway Security Features: Protecting Your Application Endpoints

Best Practices for Building Secure Serverless Microservices

Chapter 10

The Importance of Testing Microservices: Unit Testing, Integration Testing, and End-to-End Testing

- Unit Testing Lambda Functions: Ensuring Individual Function Functionality
  - Integration Testing Microservices: Verifying Communication and Data Flow
    - Testing Tools and Frameworks for Serverless Applications
- Chapter 11
  - Why Monitoring is Crucial for Serverless Applications
    - CloudWatch Logs and Metrics for Monitoring Lambda Functions
      - Application Performance Monitoring (APM) Tools for Microservices
        - Best Practices for Effective Monitoring and Debugging of Serverless Applications
- Chapter 12
  - Emerging Trends and Advancements in Serverless Technologies
    - The Future of Microservices Architecture: Continuous Innovation and Flexibility
- Conclusion
  - Appendix
    - Glossary of Key Terms

INTRODUCTION

Microservices Design Patterns for Serverless Applications: Unleash the Agile Powerhouse Within

Imagine an application that scales like a superhero, adapts like a chameleon, and costs less than a cup of coffee. That's the magic of microservices architecture, where complex applications are broken down into bite-sized, independent services.But building these microservices can feel like assembling a puzzle in a hurricane – complex, time-consuming, and prone to disaster.

Enter serverless computing, the game-changer that throws a cape on microservices and lets them soar. This book is your ultimate guide to unlocking the true potential of microservices by combining them with the power of serverless applications. Forget about managing servers, scaling infrastructure, and wrestling with deployment nightmares. With serverless, you simply focus on building amazing microservices, and the cloud handles the rest.

Why Microservices and Serverless? A Match Made in Developer Heaven

Microservices are like superheroes in their own right. Each service has a specific job, making them easier to develop, test,and deploy. They're also incredibly adaptable – if one microservice gets slammed with traffic, the rest of your application keeps humming along. But traditional microservices often require a lot of "behind-the-scenes" work – managing servers, scaling infrastructure, and dealing with operational headaches.

Here's where serverless computing swoops in like a serverless savior. With serverless, you simply upload your code and let the cloud take care of the infrastructure. You pay only for the resources you use, and scaling happens automatically. It's like having a team of invisible server ninjas working tirelessly to ensure your microservices have the resources they need, whenever they need them.

This Book: Your Microservices and Serverless Masterclass

This book is your one-stop shop for building powerful, efficient microservices applications using serverless technologies. Whether you're a seasoned developer or just starting your serverless journey, this book will equip you with the knowledge and tools you need to succeed. Here's a taste of what awaits:

- **Microservices Demystified:** We'll break down the core concepts of microservices architecture and its benefits.
- **Serverless Unveiled:** We'll explore the magic of serverless computing and how it fits perfectly into the microservices world.
- **Pattern Power:** We'll dive deep into powerful microservices design patterns specifically designed for serverless applications, like:

a. **The API Gateway Pattern:** Creating a unified entry point for your microservices.
   b. **The Event-Driven Pattern:** Building applications that react to events in real-time.
   c. **The Async Processing Pattern:** Handling long-running tasks without blocking your microservices.
   d. **The Circuit Breaker Pattern:** Ensuring your application's resilience in case of failures.
   e. **And more!**
- **Real-World Examples:** We'll bring these patterns to life with practical examples and code demonstrations, so you can see them in action.
- **Beyond the Basics:** We'll cover advanced topics like security considerations, testing strategies, and monitoring your microservices applications.

By the end of this book, you'll be a microservices and serverless master, able to build applications that are:

- **Agile:** Make changes and deploy updates quickly and efficiently.
- **Scalable:** Handle traffic spikes with ease, thanks to serverless magic.
- **Resilient:** Weather any storm with independent, fault-tolerant microservices.
- **Cost-Effective:** Pay only for the resources you use, making your application budget happy.

Ready to ditch the server headaches and unleash the power of serverless microservices? Let's dive in and unlock a whole new world of application development!

Chapter 1

The Agile Dream: Building Applications with Speed and Flexibility

In the dynamic landscape of modern software development, the demand for speed, flexibility, and scalability has never been higher. Traditional monolithic architectures often fail to meet these demands, leading to the rise of microservices and serverless architectures. Combining Agile methodologies with microservices and serverless designs empowers development teams to build applications that are both fast and flexible, capable of evolving rapidly to meet changing requirements. This article explores how these approaches synergize to create robust, efficient, and scalable applications.

Agile Methodology: The Foundation of Speed and Flexibility

Agile methodology emphasizes iterative development, continuous feedback, and collaboration. It breaks down large projects into manageable units called sprints, allowing teams to deliver functional software quickly and adapt to changes seamlessly.

Key Principles of Agile

1. Customer Collaboration Over Contract Negotiation: Engage with customers to understand their needs and gather feedback.

2. Responding to Change Over Following a Plan: Adapt to changing requirements even late in development.

3. Working Software Over Comprehensive Documentation: Prioritize delivering functional software.

4. Individuals and Interactions Over Processes and Tools: Foster effective communication within teams.

By integrating these principles, Agile ensures that development processes are streamlined, adaptable, and responsive.

Microservices: Enabling Scalability and Independent Development

Microservices architecture decomposes applications into loosely coupled, independently deployable services. Each service encapsulates a specific business function and communicates with other services through APIs.

Benefits of Microservices

1. Scalability: Individual services can be scaled independently.

2. Fault Isolation: Failures in one service do not affect others.

3. Technology Diversity: Teams can choose the best technology stack for each service.

4. Continuous Delivery: Services can be developed, tested, and deployed independently.

Designing Microservices

1. Domain-Driven Design (DDD): Align services with business domains.

2. API Gateway: Manage and route requests to appropriate services.

3. Service Discovery: Automatically locate services within the architecture.

4. Centralized Logging and Monitoring: Aggregate logs and monitor service health.

Example: Building a Microservices-Based E-commerce Application

Let's consider an e-commerce application with services for User Management, Product Catalog, Order Processing, and Payment. Each service is developed independently and communicates via RESTful APIs.

User Management Service (Python Flask)

```python
from flask import Flask, request, jsonify

app = Flask(__name__)

users = []
```

```python
@app.route('/users', methods=['POST'])
def create_user():
    user = request.json
    users.append(user)
    return jsonify(user), 201

@app.route('/users/<int:user_id>', methods=['GET'])
def get_user(user_id):
    user = next((u for u in users if u['id'] == user_id), None)
    return jsonify(user), 200 if user else 404

if __name__ == '__main__':
    app.run(port=5000)
```

Product Catalog Service (Node.js Express)

```javascript
const express = require('express');
const app = express();
app.use(express.json());
```

```
let products = [];

app.post('/products', (req, res) => {

    const product = req.body;

    products.push(product);

    res.status(201).json(product);

});

app.get('/products/:id', (req, res) => {

    const product = products.find(p => p.id == req.params.id);

    res.status(200).json(product);

});

app.listen(3000, () => {

    console.log('Product Catalog Service running on port 3000');

});
```

Order Processing Service (Java Spring Boot)

```java
```

```java
import org.springframework.boot.SpringApplication;

import org.springframework.boot.autoconfigure.SpringBootApplication;

import org.springframework.web.bind.annotation.*;

import java.util.ArrayList;

import java.util.List;

@SpringBootApplication

public class OrderServiceApplication {

    public static void main(String[] args) {

SpringApplication.run(OrderServiceApplication.class, args);

    }

@RestController

@RequestMapping("/orders")

class OrderController {

    private List<Order> orders = new ArrayList<>();

    @PostMapping
```

```java
public Order createOrder(@RequestBody Order order) {

    orders.add(order);

    return order;

}

@GetMapping("/{id}")

public Order getOrder(@PathVariable int id) {

    return orders.stream().filter(o -> o.getId() == id).findFirst().orElse(null);

}

class Order {

    private int id;

    private String product;

    private int quantity;

    // Getters and setters

}
```
```

## Payment Service (Go)
```

```go
package main

import (
    "encoding/json"
    "net/http"
)

type Payment struct {
    ID     int     `json:"id"`
    Amount float64 `json:"amount"`
}

var payments []Payment

func createPayment(w http.ResponseWriter, r *http.Request) {
    var payment Payment
    json.NewDecoder(r.Body).Decode(&payment)
    payments = append(payments, payment)
    w.WriteHeader(http.StatusCreated)
    json.NewEncoder(w).Encode(payment)
```

```go
}

func getPayment(w http.ResponseWriter, r *http.Request) {

    id := r.URL.Query().Get("id")

    for _, payment := range payments {

        if payment.ID == id {

            json.NewEncoder(w).Encode(payment)

            return

        }

        w.WriteHeader(http.StatusNotFound)

}

func main() {

    http.HandleFunc("/payments", createPayment)

    http.HandleFunc("/payments", getPayment)

    http.ListenAndServe(":8080", nil)

}
```
```

## Communication Between Services
```

Services communicate through RESTful APIs. An API Gateway can route external requests to the appropriate internal services, providing a single entry point for the application.

Serverless Architectures: Maximizing Agility and Cost Efficiency

Serverless computing abstracts server management, allowing developers to focus on code and functionality. Functions are executed in response to events, scaling automatically based on demand.

Benefits of Serverless

1. Reduced Operational Overhead: No need to manage infrastructure.

2. Automatic Scaling: Functions scale in response to demand.

3. Cost Efficiency: Pay only for actual usage.

4. Rapid Deployment: Functions can be deployed independently.

Serverless Design Patterns

1. Function-as-a-Service (FaaS): Break down application logic into individual functions.

2. Event-Driven Architecture: Trigger functions based on events (e.g., HTTP requests, database changes).

3. Backend-as-a-Service (BaaS): Use third-party services for backend functionality (e.g., authentication, databases).

Example: Building a Serverless E-commerce Application

Using AWS Lambda, API Gateway, and DynamoDB, we can create a serverless e-commerce application.

User Management Function (AWS Lambda with Python)

```python
import json
import boto3

dynamodb = boto3.resource('dynamodb')
table = dynamodb.Table('Users')

def lambda_handler(event, context):
    if event['httpMethod'] == 'POST':
        user = json.loads(event['body'])
        table.put_item(Item=user)
        return {
            'statusCode': 201,
```

```
        'body': json.dumps(user)
    }
    elif event['httpMethod'] == 'GET':
        user_id = event['pathParameters']['id']
        response = table.get_item(Key={'id': user_id})
        return {
            'statusCode': 200,
            'body': json.dumps(response['Item'])
        }
```

Product Catalog Function (AWS Lambda with Node.js)

```javascript
const AWS = require('aws-sdk');

const dynamodb = new AWS.DynamoDB.DocumentClient();

exports.handler = async (event) => {
    if (event.httpMethod === 'POST') {
```

```
    const product = JSON.parse(event.body);
    await dynamodb.put({
      TableName: 'Products',
      Item: product
    }).promise();
    return {
      statusCode: 201,
      body: JSON.stringify(product)
    };
} else if (event.httpMethod === 'GET') {
    const productId = event.pathParameters.id;
    const result = await dynamodb.get({
      TableName: 'Products',
      Key: { id: productId }
    }).promise();
    return {
      statusCode: 200,
```

        body: JSON.stringify(result.Item)

   };

```

### Order Processing Function (AWS Lambda with Java)

```java

import com.amazonaws.services.lambda.runtime.Context;

import com.amazonaws.services.lambda.runtime.RequestHandler;

import com.amazonaws.services.dynamodbv2.AmazonDynamoDB;

import com.amazonaws.services.dynamodbv2.AmazonDynamoDBClientBuilder;

import com.amazonaws.services.dynamodbv2.document.DynamoDB;

import com.amazonaws.services.dynamodbv2.document.Table;

import com.fasterxml.jackson.databind.ObjectMapper;

```java
import java.util.Map;

public class OrderHandler implements
RequestHandler<Map<String, Object>,
ApiGatewayResponse> {

    private static final AmazonDynamoDB client =
    AmazonDynamoDBClientBuilder.defaultClient();

    private static final DynamoDB dynamoDB = new
    DynamoDB(client);

    private static final Table table =
    dynamoDB.getTable("Orders");

    private static final ObjectMapper mapper = new
    ObjectMapper();

    @Override
    public ApiGatewayResponse
    handleRequest(Map<String, Object> event, Context
    context) {

        if ("POST".equals(event.get("httpMethod"))) {

            Map<String, Object> order = (Map<String,
    Object>) event.get("body");

            table.putItem(new Item().withPrimaryKey("id",
    order.get("id")).withMap("order", order));

            return ApiGatewayResponse.builder()
```

```java
                    .setStatusCode(201)

                    .setObjectBody(order)

                    .build();

        } else if ("GET".equals(event.get("httpMethod"))) {

            String orderId = (String) ((Map<String, String>) event.get("pathParameters")).get("id");

            Item item = table.getItem("id", orderId);

            if (item == null) {

                return ApiGatewayResponse.builder()

                    .setStatusCode(404)

                    .build();

            }

            return ApiGatewayResponse.builder()

                    .setStatusCode(200)

                    .setObjectBody(item.asMap())

                    .build();

        }

        return ApiGatewayResponse.builder()
```

```
            .setStatusCode(400)

        .build();

    }
```
```

## Communication and Orchestration

In a serverless architecture, services communicate through APIs managed by API Gateway. Each Lambda function can be triggered by HTTP requests, changes in the database, or other events, promoting loose coupling and independent scaling.

## Integrating Agile with Microservices and Serverless Architectures

Combining Agile methodologies with microservices and serverless architectures enhances the ability to deliver applications quickly and adapt to changes. Here's how:

**1. Iterative Development:** Agile's sprint cycles align well with the independent development of microservices and serverless functions, enabling continuous delivery and integration.

**2. Continuous Feedback:** Microservices and serverless architectures allow for rapid iteration and deployment, making it easier to incorporate user feedback and adapt to changing requirements.
```

3. Collaboration: Agile's emphasis on collaboration is supported by microservices' division of services, allowing teams to work on different services concurrently without stepping on each other's toes.

Example Agile Workflow

1. Planning: Define the features and functionality to be developed in the upcoming sprint. Break down tasks into user stories.

2. Development: Assign user stories to team members who will implement them as microservices or serverless functions.

3. Testing: Continuously integrate and test the services/functions developed during the sprint.

4. Review: Conduct sprint reviews to gather feedback and identify areas for improvement.

5. Deployment: Deploy the services/functions to production, ensuring they are scalable and reliable.

CI/CD Pipeline

A Continuous Integration and Continuous Deployment (CI/CD) pipeline is crucial for automating the build, test, and deployment processes. Here's an example using AWS services:

1. CodeCommit: Store your source code in AWS CodeCommit.

2. CodeBuild: Use AWS CodeBuild to build and test your code.

3. CodePipeline: Automate the CI/CD pipeline using AWS CodePipeline.

4. Lambda Deployment: Deploy your Lambda functions using AWS CodeDeploy.

The synergy between Agile methodologies, microservices architecture, and serverless computing creates a powerful paradigm for modern software development. Agile provides the framework for iterative, responsive development. Microservices offer the scalability and flexibility to handle complex, evolving applications. Serverless computing maximizes efficiency by abstracting infrastructure management and allowing developers to focus on code.

By integrating these approaches, development teams can achieve unprecedented speed and flexibility, meeting the demands of today's fast-paced, ever-changing technological landscape. This Agile dream of building applications with speed and flexibility is not just an ideal but a practical, achievable reality through thoughtful design and implementation.

The Microservices Revolution: Breaking Down the Monolith

The world of software development is experiencing a paradigm shift. The monolithic approach, which once dominated the industry, is being replaced by microservices architecture. This transition is not just a trend but a revolution, driven by the need for scalability, flexibility, and faster time-to-market. In this article, we will explore the principles of microservices, their benefits, and how they can be implemented using serverless architectures. We'll also delve into design patterns that ensure robust, maintainable, and scalable applications.

The Monolithic Legacy

Traditional monolithic applications are built as a single, indivisible unit. While this approach simplifies initial development, it introduces significant challenges as applications grow:

1. Scalability Issues: Scaling a monolith means replicating the entire application, even if only one component is under heavy load.

2. Limited Flexibility: Changes in one part of the application can impact the entire system, making updates risky and time-consuming.

3. Slow Development: Large codebases are difficult to manage, slowing down the development process and making continuous integration challenging.

4. Fault Isolation: A failure in one part of the application can bring down the entire system.

Enter Microservices

Microservices architecture addresses these issues by decomposing applications into smaller, independent services. Each service encapsulates a specific business function and can be developed, deployed, and scaled independently.

Key Principles of Microservices

1. Single Responsibility Principle: Each service focuses on a single functionality.

2. Decentralized Data Management: Services manage their own databases, enhancing modularity.

3. API-First Design: Services communicate through well-defined APIs.

4. Independent Deployment: Services can be deployed independently, facilitating continuous delivery.

Benefits of Microservices

1. Scalability: Scale individual services based on demand.

2. Resilience: Isolate failures to prevent cascading issues.

3. Technology Diversity: Use the best technology stack for each service.

4. Faster Development: Smaller codebases and independent teams speed up the development process.

Microservices in Serverless Architectures

Serverless computing further enhances microservices by abstracting infrastructure management. Developers focus solely on writing code while the cloud provider handles the underlying infrastructure.

Benefits of Serverless

1. Automatic Scaling: Functions scale automatically based on demand.

2. Cost Efficiency: Pay only for actual usage, reducing costs.

3. Reduced Operational Overhead: No need to manage servers or infrastructure.

4. Rapid Deployment: Deploy functions independently and quickly.

Serverless Microservices Design Patterns

Several design patterns are crucial for building effective microservices in a serverless environment:

1. Function-as-a-Service (FaaS): Decompose application logic into stateless functions.

2. API Gateway: Use an API Gateway to route requests to the appropriate functions.

3. Event-Driven Architecture: Trigger functions based on events (e.g., HTTP requests, database changes).

4. Backend-as-a-Service (BaaS): Leverage third-party services for backend functionalities like authentication and databases.

Example: E-commerce Application

Let's illustrate the microservices approach using an example of an e-commerce application. We'll create services for User Management, Product Catalog, Order Processing, and Payment. These services will be implemented using AWS Lambda (serverless functions) and DynamoDB (NoSQL database).

User Management Service (AWS Lambda with Python)

```python
import json

import boto3

from boto3.dynamodb.conditions import Key

dynamodb = boto3.resource('dynamodb')

table = dynamodb.Table('Users')

def lambda_handler(event, context):

    if event['httpMethod'] == 'POST':

        user = json.loads(event['body'])
```

```
        table.put_item(Item=user)

        return {

            'statusCode': 201,

            'body': json.dumps(user)

        }

    elif event['httpMethod'] == 'GET':

        user_id = event['pathParameters']['id']

        response = table.get_item(Key={'id': user_id})

        return {

            'statusCode': 200 if 'Item' in response else 404,

            'body': json.dumps(response.get('Item', {}))

        }
```

Product Catalog Service (AWS Lambda with Node.js)

```javascript
const AWS = require('aws-sdk');
```

```javascript
const dynamodb = new AWS.DynamoDB.DocumentClient();

exports.handler = async (event) => {

    if (event.httpMethod === 'POST') {

        const product = JSON.parse(event.body);

        await dynamodb.put({

            TableName: 'Products',

            Item: product

        }).promise();

        return {

            statusCode: 201,

            body: JSON.stringify(product)

        };

    } else if (event.httpMethod === 'GET') {

        const productId = event.pathParameters.id;

        const result = await dynamodb.get({

            TableName: 'Products',

            Key: { id: productId }
```

```
        }).promise();
        return {
            statusCode: 200,
            body: JSON.stringify(result.Items)
        };
};
```

Order Processing Service (AWS Lambda with Java)

```java
import com.amazonaws.services.lambda.runtime.Context;

import com.amazonaws.services.lambda.runtime.RequestHandler;

import com.amazonaws.services.dynamodbv2.AmazonDynamoDB;

import com.amazonaws.services.dynamodbv2.AmazonDynamoDBClientBuilder;

import com.amazonaws.services.dynamodbv2.document.DynamoDB;
```

```java
import com.amazonaws.services.dynamodbv2.document.Table;

import com.amazonaws.services.dynamodbv2.document.Item;

import com.fasterxml.jackson.databind.ObjectMapper;

import java.util.Map;

public class OrderHandler implements RequestHandler<Map<String, Object>, ApiGatewayResponse> {

    private static final AmazonDynamoDB client = AmazonDynamoDBClientBuilder.defaultClient();

    private static final DynamoDB dynamoDB = new DynamoDB(client);

    private static final Table table = dynamoDB.getTable("Orders");

    private static final ObjectMapper mapper = new ObjectMapper();

    @Override
    public ApiGatewayResponse handleRequest(Map<String, Object> event, Context context) {

        if ("POST".equals(event.get("httpMethod"))) {
```

```java
        try {

            Map<String, Object> order =
mapper.readValue((String) event.get("body"),
Map.class);

            Item item = new Item().withPrimaryKey("id",
order.get("id")).withMap("order", order);

            table.putItem(item);

            return ApiGatewayResponse.builder()

                .setStatusCode(201)

                .setObjectBody(order)

                .build();

        } catch (Exception e) {

            return ApiGatewayResponse.builder()

                .setStatusCode(500)

                .setObjectBody(e.getMessage())

                .build();

        }

    } else if ("GET".equals(event.get("httpMethod"))) {
```

```java
        String orderId = (String) ((Map<String, String>) event.get("pathParameters")).get("id");

        Item item = table.getItem("id", orderId);

        if (item == null) {

            return ApiGatewayResponse.builder()

                    .setStatusCode(404)

                    .build();

        }

        return ApiGatewayResponse.builder()

                .setStatusCode(200)

                .setObjectBody(item.asMap())

                .build();

    }

    return ApiGatewayResponse.builder()

            .setStatusCode(400)

            .build();

}
```
```
...
```

Payment Service (AWS Lambda with Go)

```go
package main

import (
    "encoding/json"
    "net/http"
    "github.com/aws/aws-lambda-go/events"
    "github.com/aws/aws-lambda-go/lambda"
    "github.com/aws/aws-sdk-go/aws"
    "github.com/aws/aws-sdk-go/aws/session"
    "github.com/aws/aws-sdk-go/service/dynamodb"
)

type Payment struct {
    ID     string  `json:"id"`
    Amount float64 `json:"amount"`
}

var (
```

```go
        sess = session.Must(session.NewSession())

        db   = dynamodb.New(sess)
)

func createPayment(request events.APIGatewayProxyRequest) (events.APIGatewayProxyResponse, error) {

    var payment Payment

    json.Unmarshal([]byte(request.Body), &payment)

    item, err := dynamodb.MarshalMap(payment)

    if err != nil {

        return events.APIGatewayProxyResponse{StatusCode: 500}, err

    }

    _, err = db.PutItem(&dynamodb.PutItemInput{

        TableName: aws.String("Payments"),

        Item:      item,

    })

    if err != nil {
```

```go
        return
events.APIGatewayProxyResponse{StatusCode: 500},
err

    }

    return events.APIGatewayProxyResponse{

        StatusCode: 201,

        Body:      string(request.Body),

    }, nil

}

func getPayment(request
events.APIGatewayProxyRequest)
(events.APIGatewayProxyResponse, error) {

    paymentID := request.PathParameters["id"]

    result, err := db.GetItem(&dynamodb.GetItemInput{

        TableName: aws.String("Payments"),

        Key: map[string]*dynamodb.AttributeValue{

            "id": {S: aws.String(paymentID)},

        },

    if err != nil || result.Item == nil {
```

```go
		return events.APIGatewayProxyResponse{StatusCode: 404}, nil
	}

	payment := Payment{}

	err = dynamodb.UnmarshalMap(result.Item, &payment)

	if err != nil {
		return events.APIGatewayProxyResponse{StatusCode: 500}, err
	}

	body, err := json.Marshal(payment)

	if err != nil {
		return events.APIGatewayProxyResponse{StatusCode: 500}, err
	}

	return events.APIGatewayProxyResponse{
		StatusCode: 200,
```

```
        Body:    string(body),
    }, nil
}

func main() {

    lambda.Start(func(request events.APIGatewayProxyRequest) (events.APIGatewayProxyResponse, error) {

        switch request.HTTPMethod {

        case "POST":

            return createPayment(request)

        case "GET":

            return getPayment(request)

        default:

            return events.APIGatewayProxyResponse{StatusCode: 400}, nil

        }
```
```

## Communication and Orchestration
```

In a serverless microservices architecture, services communicate through APIs managed by an API Gateway. Each Lambda function can be triggered by HTTP requests, changes in the database, or other events, promoting loose coupling and independent scaling.

API Gateway

An API Gateway serves as a single entry point for client requests, routing them to the appropriate microservices. It can handle authentication, request validation, and rate limiting, ensuring secure and efficient communication.

Event-Driven Architecture

Serverless microservices often rely on event-driven patterns. For instance, an order placement might trigger events that invoke the Payment Service and update the Order Processing Service. This decoupling ensures that services remain autonomous and scalable.

CI/CD Pipeline

A Continuous Integration and Continuous Deployment (CI/CD) pipeline automates the build, test, and deployment processes. For serverless applications, tools like AWS CodePipeline, CodeBuild, and CodeDeploy can be used.

1. CodeCommit: Store your source code in AWS CodeCommit.

2. CodeBuild: Use AWS CodeBuild to build and test your code.

3. CodePipeline: Automate the CI/CD pipeline using AWS CodePipeline.

4. Lambda Deployment: Deploy your Lambda functions using AWS CodeDeploy.

Example CI/CD Workflow

1. Commit Code: Developers commit code changes to a repository in CodeCommit.

2. Build and Test: CodeBuild compiles the code, runs tests, and generates build artifacts.

3. Deploy: CodePipeline deploys the artifacts to Lambda, updating the functions.

YAML Example for CodePipeline

```yaml
version: 0.2

phases:
  install:
    runtime-versions:
      python: 3.8
```

```
  build:

    commands:

      - pip install -r requirements.txt

  post_build:

    commands:

      - aws cloudformation package --template-file template.yml --s3-bucket my-bucket --output-template-file output.yml

artifacts:

  type: zip

  files:

    - output.yml
```

Monitoring and Logging

Effective monitoring and logging are crucial for maintaining and debugging microservices. AWS CloudWatch provides comprehensive monitoring, logging, and alerting capabilities.

CloudWatch Configuration

1. Logs: Capture logs from Lambda functions.

2. Metrics: Monitor function invocations, durations, and errors.

3. Alarms: Set up alarms to notify when thresholds are breached.

```python
import logging

logger = logging.getLogger()

logger.setLevel(logging.INFO)

def lambda_handler(event, context):

    logger.info("Received event: %s", json.dumps(event))

    # Function logic here
```

The shift from monolithic to microservices architecture represents a significant evolution in software development. By decomposing applications into smaller, independently deployable services, microservices provide unparalleled scalability, flexibility, and resilience. When combined with serverless computing, the benefits are further amplified, offering automatic scaling, cost efficiency, and reduced operational overhead.

Microservices, when designed with patterns like API Gateway, event-driven architecture, and Backend-as-a-

Service, allow developers to build robust, maintainable, and scalable applications. The integration of CI/CD pipelines ensures continuous delivery, enabling rapid iteration and deployment.

The microservices revolution, supported by serverless architectures, empowers development teams to break down the monolith, build applications with speed and flexibility, and meet the ever-evolving demands of the modern software landscape.

Embrace the microservices revolution and leverage serverless architectures to transform your software development processes. The future of agile, scalable, and resilient applications is here.

The Serverless Game Changer: Unleashing Microservices from Infrastructure Woes

The evolution of software development paradigms has brought about significant transformations, and one of the most impactful changes is the rise of serverless computing. By enabling developers to focus on writing code without worrying about infrastructure management, serverless computing has unleashed the potential of microservices architecture, making it easier to develop, deploy, and scale applications. This article explores how serverless computing acts as a game changer for microservices, examining various design patterns and illustrating with code examples how to implement serverless microservices effectively.

Understanding Serverless Computing and Microservices

What is Serverless Computing?

Serverless computing is a cloud-computing model where the cloud provider automatically manages the infrastructure required to run code. Developers write functions, which are executed in response to events, and the cloud provider handles the provisioning, scaling, and management of servers. This allows developers to focus solely on business logic, reducing operational overhead and improving agility.

What are Microservices?

Microservices architecture is a design approach where a single application is composed of multiple loosely coupled, independently deployable services. Each service encapsulates a specific business capability and communicates with other services through well-defined APIs, usually over HTTP or messaging queues.

The Synergy of Serverless and Microservices

Combining serverless computing with microservices architecture offers numerous benefits:

- **Scalability**: Serverless platforms automatically scale functions based on demand.
- **Cost Efficiency**: Pay-per-use pricing models ensure that you only pay for the actual execution time of your functions.

- **Reduced Operational Complexity**: Serverless abstracts the underlying infrastructure, allowing developers to focus on code and business logic.
- **Faster Development Cycles**: Independent microservices can be developed, tested, and deployed without affecting the entire system.

Serverless Microservices Design Patterns

To harness the full potential of serverless microservices, developers can leverage various design patterns. These patterns address common challenges and provide best practices for building robust and scalable serverless applications.

1. Function as a Service (FaaS)

The fundamental building block of serverless applications is the FaaS pattern. Functions are triggered by specific events and execute single units of work. AWS Lambda, Azure Functions, and Google Cloud Functions are popular implementations of this pattern.

```python
# Example AWS Lambda function in Python

import json

def lambda_handler(event, context):
    # Business logic here
```

```
    result = {"message": "Hello, Serverless Microservices!"}

    return {
        'statusCode': 200,
        'body': json.dumps(result)
    }
```

2. API Gateway Pattern

The API Gateway pattern is essential for exposing microservices through RESTful APIs. An API Gateway acts as a reverse proxy, routing client requests to appropriate backend services. It can handle tasks such as authentication, authorization, and rate limiting.

```yaml
# Example AWS API Gateway configuration (serverless.yml)

service: serverless-microservices

provider:
  name: aws
  runtime: python3.8
```

```
functions:
  hello:
    handler: handler.lambda_handler
    events:
      - http:
          path: hello
          method: get
resources:
  Resources:
    ApiGatewayRestApi:
      Type: 'AWS::ApiGateway::RestApi'
      Properties:
        Name: 'ServerlessMicroservicesAPI'
```

3. Event-Driven Architecture

In a serverless environment, event-driven architecture is a powerful pattern for decoupling services. Events trigger functions, facilitating asynchronous communication between microservices. This pattern is often implemented using services like AWS SNS (Simple Notification Service) and SQS (Simple Queue Service).

```python
# Example AWS Lambda function triggered by SQS

import json

import boto3

sqs = boto3.client('sqs')

def lambda_handler(event, context):

    for record in event['Records']:

        message_body = json.loads(record['body'])

        process_message(message_body)

def process_message(message):

    print(f"Processing message: {message}")

    # Business logic here
```

4. Saga Pattern

The Saga pattern manages distributed transactions across microservices. It ensures data consistency and handles rollbacks by coordinating a series of local transactions. In a serverless context, step functions or state machines can implement this pattern.

```json
{
  "Comment": "A sample saga for order processing",
  "StartAt": "CreateOrder",
  "States": {
    "CreateOrder": {
      "Type": "Task",
      "Resource": "arn:aws:lambda:us-east-1:123456789012:function:CreateOrderFunction",
      "Next": "ReserveInventory"
    },
    "ReserveInventory": {
      "Type": "Task",
      "Resource": "arn:aws:lambda:us-east-1:123456789012:function:ReserveInventoryFunction",
      "Next": "ProcessPayment"
```

      },

  "ProcessPayment": {

   "Type": "Task",

   "Resource": "arn:aws:lambda:us-east-1:123456789012:function:ProcessPaymentFunction",

   "End": true

  }
```

## 5. Circuit Breaker Pattern

To prevent cascading failures in a microservices architecture, the Circuit Breaker pattern helps to gracefully degrade service performance during outages. In a serverless setup, AWS API Gateway and Lambda can be configured to implement circuit breakers.

```python

# Example Circuit Breaker with retries in a Lambda function

import requests

from requests.exceptions import HTTPError

def lambda_handler(event, context):

```
url = "https://example.com/api/resource"
try:
    response = requests.get(url)
    response.raise_for_status()
    return response.json()
except HTTPError as http_err:
    print(f"HTTP error occurred: {http_err}")
    raise
except Exception as err:
    print(f"Other error occurred: {err}")
    raise
```

6. Fan-out/Fan-in Pattern

The Fan-out/Fan-in pattern processes tasks in parallel by distributing workloads across multiple functions. This pattern is useful for data processing pipelines and can be implemented using AWS Lambda with SNS or SQS.

```python
# Example Fan-out with AWS Lambda and SNS
```

```python
import json

import boto3

sns = boto3.client('sns')

def lambda_handler(event, context):
    message = {"task": "process_data"}
    sns.publish(
        TopicArn='arn:aws:sns:us-east-1:123456789012:MyTopic',
        Message=json.dumps(message)
    )

# Example Fan-in with AWS Lambda and SQS
def lambda_handler(event, context):
    for record in event['Records']:
        message_body = json.loads(record['body'])
        process_message(message_body)

def process_message(message):
    print(f"Processing message: {message}")
    # Business logic here
```

```

Serverless computing has indeed become a game changer for microservices architecture. By abstracting infrastructure management, it allows developers to focus on building and deploying business logic rapidly and efficiently. The combination of serverless and microservices offers unmatched scalability, cost efficiency, and reduced operational complexity.

Employing design patterns like FaaS, API Gateway, event-driven architecture, Saga, Circuit Breaker, and Fan-out/Fan-in can help developers build robust, resilient, and scalable serverless applications. As serverless technology continues to evolve, its integration with microservices will undoubtedly pave the way for even more innovative and efficient software solutions.

## Why Serverless and Microservices? A Perfect Match for Agile Development

In today's fast-paced digital landscape, agility in software development is not just an advantage but a necessity. Organizations seek to deliver features and improvements rapidly to stay competitive. To achieve this, many are turning to the powerful combination of serverless computing and microservices architecture. This article explores why serverless and microservices are a perfect match for agile development, highlighting various design patterns and providing code examples to illustrate their implementation.

**The Need for Agility in Development**
```

Agile development emphasizes iterative progress, collaboration, and flexibility to respond to changing requirements. Traditional monolithic architectures often struggle to meet these demands due to their complexity and lack of modularity. By contrast, microservices architecture breaks down applications into small, independently deployable services, each handling a specific business function. This modularity aligns well with agile principles, allowing for faster development, testing, and deployment cycles.

Serverless Computing: An Agile Enabler

Serverless computing further enhances agility by abstracting away infrastructure management. Developers can focus solely on writing code while cloud providers handle provisioning, scaling, and maintenance of servers. This shift not only reduces operational overhead but also accelerates the development process. Serverless platforms like AWS Lambda, Azure Functions, and Google Cloud Functions allow developers to deploy code as individual functions that execute in response to events.

Benefits of Serverless and Microservices for Agile Development

1. Scalability: Serverless platforms automatically scale functions based on demand, ensuring that applications can handle varying loads without manual intervention.

2. Cost Efficiency: Pay-per-use pricing models mean you only pay for the actual execution time of your functions, reducing costs associated with idle resources.

3. Reduced Operational Complexity: By abstracting infrastructure management, serverless computing allows developers to focus on delivering business value.

4. Faster Time-to-Market: Independent microservices can be developed, tested, and deployed rapidly, enabling quicker releases and iterations.

5. Improved Resilience: Microservices are inherently decoupled, so failures in one service do not necessarily impact the entire system.

Design Patterns for Serverless Microservices

To effectively leverage serverless computing and microservices architecture, developers can employ various design patterns. These patterns address common challenges and provide best practices for building scalable and resilient serverless applications.

1. Function as a Service (FaaS)

At the core of serverless applications is the FaaS pattern. Functions are designed to handle specific tasks and are triggered by events. This pattern encourages modular, single-responsibility functions that are easy to develop, test, and deploy.

```python
```

```python
# Example AWS Lambda function in Python
import json

def lambda_handler(event, context):
    # Business logic here
    result = {"message": "Hello, Serverless Microservices!"}
    return {
        'statusCode': 200,
        'body': json.dumps(result)
    }
```

2. API Gateway Pattern

The API Gateway pattern involves using an API Gateway to expose microservices through RESTful APIs. An API Gateway acts as a reverse proxy, routing client requests to the appropriate backend services. It also handles tasks such as authentication, authorization, and rate limiting.

```yaml
# Example AWS API Gateway configuration (serverless.yml)
```

```yaml
service: serverless-microservices

provider:
  name: aws
  runtime: python3.8

functions:
  hello:
    handler: handler.lambda_handler
    events:
      - http:
          path: hello
          method: get

resources:
  Resources:
    ApiGatewayRestApi:
      Type: 'AWS::ApiGateway::RestApi'
      Properties:
        Name: 'ServerlessMicroservicesAPI'
```

```

## 3. Event-Driven Architecture

Event-driven architecture is a powerful pattern for decoupling services in a serverless environment. Functions are triggered by events, enabling asynchronous communication between microservices. This pattern is often implemented using services like AWS SNS (Simple Notification Service) and SQS (Simple Queue Service).

```python
# Example AWS Lambda function triggered by SQS
import json
import boto3

sqs = boto3.client('sqs')

def lambda_handler(event, context):
    for record in event['Records']:
        message_body = json.loads(record['body'])
        process_message(message_body)

def process_message(message):
    print(f"Processing message: {message}")
```
```

```
    # Business logic here
```

4. Saga Pattern

The Saga pattern manages distributed transactions across microservices, ensuring data consistency and handling rollbacks. In a serverless context, this pattern can be implemented using state machines or step functions.

```json
{
  "Comment": "A sample saga for order processing",
  "StartAt": "CreateOrder",
  "States": {
    "CreateOrder": {
      "Type": "Task",
      "Resource": "arn:aws:lambda:us-east-1:123456789012:function:CreateOrderFunction",
      "Next": "ReserveInventory"
    },
    "ReserveInventory": {
```

```
    "Type": "Task",
    "Resource": "arn:aws:lambda:us-east-1:123456789012:function:ReserveInventoryFunction",
    "Next": "ProcessPayment"
},
"ProcessPayment": {
    "Type": "Task",
    "Resource": "arn:aws:lambda:us-east-1:123456789012:function:ProcessPaymentFunction",
    "End": true
}
```

5. Circuit Breaker Pattern

The Circuit Breaker pattern helps to prevent cascading failures by gracefully degrading service performance during outages. In a serverless setup, services like AWS API Gateway and Lambda can be configured to implement circuit breakers.

```python
# Example Circuit Breaker with retries in a Lambda function
```

```
import requests
from requests.exceptions import HTTPError
def lambda_handler(event, context):
    url = "https://example.com/api/resource"
    try:
        response = requests.get(url)
        response.raise_for_status()
        return response.json()
    except HTTPError as http_err:
        print(f"HTTP error occurred: {http_err}")
        raise
    except Exception as err:
        print(f"Other error occurred: {err}")
        raise
```

6. Fan-out/Fan-in Pattern

The Fan-out/Fan-in pattern processes tasks in parallel by distributing workloads across multiple functions. This pattern is useful for data processing pipelines and can be implemented using AWS Lambda with SNS or SQS.

```python
# Example Fan-out with AWS Lambda and SNS
import json
import boto3

sns = boto3.client('sns')

def lambda_handler(event, context):
    message = {"task": "process_data"}
    sns.publish(
        TopicArn='arn:aws:sns:us-east-1:123456789012:MyTopic',
        Message=json.dumps(message)
    )

# Example Fan-in with AWS Lambda and SQS
def lambda_handler(event, context):
    for record in event['Records']:
        message_body = json.loads(record['body'])
```

```
    process_message(message_body)

def process_message(message):

    print(f"Processing message: {message}")

    # Business logic here
```
```

The combination of serverless computing and microservices architecture is a natural fit for agile development. Serverless platforms abstract infrastructure management, enabling developers to focus on writing code and delivering business value. Microservices architecture promotes modularity, independent deployment, and resilience, all of which align perfectly with agile principles.

By leveraging design patterns such as FaaS, API Gateway, event-driven architecture, Saga, Circuit Breaker, and Fan-out/Fan-in, developers can build robust, scalable, and resilient serverless applications. These patterns address common challenges and provide best practices for effective implementation.

As the demand for agility in software development continues to grow, the synergy between serverless computing and microservices will undoubtedly play a critical role in shaping the future of application development. This powerful combination not only accelerates time-to-market but also enhances the overall
```

quality and resilience of software solutions, making it an indispensable approach for modern development teams.

Chapter 2

Core Concepts of Microservices: A Service-Oriented Approach

Microservices architecture has emerged as a robust solution to the limitations of traditional monolithic systems. This approach breaks down applications into a suite of small, independent services, each encapsulating a specific business function. These services communicate with each other through well-defined APIs, typically using HTTP or messaging protocols. When combined with serverless computing, microservices become even more powerful, providing enhanced scalability, reduced operational complexity, and faster time-to-market. This article delves into the core concepts of microservices, illustrating how they can be implemented using serverless design patterns.

What are Microservices?

Microservices are a design approach where an application is composed of multiple, loosely coupled services. Each service focuses on a specific business capability, runs its own process, and can be deployed independently. This architecture promotes a modular approach to development, allowing teams to work on different services simultaneously, leading to increased agility and faster delivery of new features.

Key Characteristics of Microservices

1. Independence: Each microservice is independently deployable and scalable.

2. Single Responsibility: Services are designed around business capabilities and each service does one thing well.

3. Decentralized Data Management: Each microservice manages its own database or data storage.

4. Communication: Services communicate via APIs or messaging systems.

5. Automated Deployment: Continuous integration and continuous deployment (CI/CD) are integral to microservices.

Core Concepts of Microservices

1. Service Independence

The primary advantage of microservices is their independence. Each service is a standalone component that can be developed, deployed, and scaled independently of other services. This separation allows for better fault isolation; if one service fails, it does not affect the entire system.

```python

# Example AWS Lambda function for a User Service

import json
```

```python
import boto3
dynamodb = boto3.resource('dynamodb')
table = dynamodb.Table('Users')
def lambda_handler(event, context):
    user_id = event['pathParameters']['id']
    response = table.get_item(Key={'user_id': user_id})
    if 'Item' in response:
        return {
            'statusCode': 200,
            'body': json.dumps(response['Item'])
        }
    else:
        return {
            'statusCode': 404,
            'body': json.dumps({'error': 'User not found'})
        }
```

2. API Gateway Pattern

An API Gateway acts as the entry point for client requests to a microservices-based application. It routes requests to the appropriate services, handles authentication, and manages rate limiting. This pattern simplifies client interactions and improves security.

```yaml
# Example API Gateway configuration for serverless (serverless.yml)

service: user-service

provider:
  name: aws
  runtime: python3.8

functions:
  getUser:
    handler: handler.lambda_handler
    events:
      - http:
          path: users/{id}
          method: get
```

```

## 3. Decentralized Data Management

In microservices architecture, each service has its own database, which allows for more flexible data models and scalability. This approach prevents the tight coupling associated with a single, centralized database.

```python
# Example AWS Lambda function for an Order Service
import json
import boto3

dynamodb = boto3.resource('dynamodb')
table = dynamodb.Table('Orders')

def lambda_handler(event, context):
    order_id = event['pathParameters']['id']
    response = table.get_item(Key={'order_id': order_id})
    if 'Item' in response:
        return {
            'statusCode': 200,
            'body': json.dumps(response['Item'])

```
        }
    else:
        return {
            'statusCode': 404,
            'body': json.dumps({'error': 'Order not found'})
        }
```

4. Event-Driven Architecture

Event-driven architecture is a cornerstone of microservices, enabling asynchronous communication between services. Events trigger functions, decoupling services and allowing them to operate independently. AWS SNS (Simple Notification Service) and SQS (Simple Queue Service) are commonly used for this pattern.

```python
# Example AWS Lambda function triggered by SNS
import json
import boto3

sns = boto3.client('sns')
```

```python
def lambda_handler(event, context):
    message = {
        "event": "user_created",
        "user_id": "12345"
    }
    sns.publish(
        TopicArn='arn:aws:sns:us-east-1:123456789012:UserEvents',
        Message=json.dumps(message)
    )
```

5. Saga Pattern

The Saga pattern manages complex transactions across multiple microservices. Each service performs a local transaction and publishes events to trigger the next step. If a step fails, compensating transactions are triggered to rollback the changes.

```json
{
  "Comment": "Order processing saga",
```

```
"StartAt": "CreateOrder",

"States": {

  "CreateOrder": {

    "Type": "Task",

    "Resource": "arn:aws:lambda:us-east-1:123456789012:function:CreateOrder",

    "Next": "ReserveInventory"

  },

  "ReserveInventory": {

    "Type": "Task",

    "Resource": "arn:aws:lambda:us-east-1:123456789012:function:ReserveInventory",

    "Next": "ProcessPayment"

  },

  "ProcessPayment": {

    "Type": "Task",

    "Resource": "arn:aws:lambda:us-east-1:123456789012:function:ProcessPayment",

    "End": true
```

}
```

## 6. Circuit Breaker Pattern

The Circuit Breaker pattern prevents cascading failures in microservices architecture by monitoring service interactions and stopping requests to a failing service. This helps to isolate faults and improve overall system resilience.

```python
# Example Circuit Breaker implementation in a Lambda function

import requests
from requests.exceptions import HTTPError

def lambda_handler(event, context):
    url = "https://example.com/api/resource"
    try:
        response = requests.get(url)
        response.raise_for_status()
        return response.json()
    except HTTPError as http_err:

```
        print(f"HTTP error occurred: {http_err}")

        raise

    except Exception as err:

        print(f"Other error occurred: {err}")

        raise
```

7. Fan-out/Fan-in Pattern

The Fan-out/Fan-in pattern distributes tasks across multiple services for parallel processing and then aggregates the results. This pattern is useful for data processing and analysis tasks.

```python
# Example Fan-out with AWS Lambda and SNS

import json

import boto3

sns = boto3.client('sns')

def lambda_handler(event, context):

    message = {"task": "process_data"}

    sns.publish(
```

```
        TopicArn='arn:aws:sns:us-east-1:123456789012:DataProcessing',

        Message=json.dumps(message)

    )

# Example Fan-in with AWS Lambda and SQS

def lambda_handler(event, context):

    for record in event['Records']:

        message_body = json.loads(record['body'])

        process_message(message_body)

def process_message(message):

    print(f"Processing message: {message}")

    # Business logic here

```

Microservices architecture, enhanced by serverless computing, provides a powerful and flexible framework for building modern applications. The core concepts of microservices—service independence, API Gateway, decentralized data management, event-driven architecture, Saga, Circuit Breaker, and Fan-out/Fan-in patterns—enable developers to create scalable, resilient, and agile systems.

By embracing these principles and leveraging serverless technologies, organizations can reduce operational complexity, accelerate development cycles, and improve fault isolation. The modularity and independence of microservices, combined with the abstraction of serverless infrastructure, make this approach particularly suited for the dynamic and evolving demands of today's software development landscape. As the industry continues to evolve, the synergy between microservices and serverless computing will undoubtedly drive further innovation and efficiency in building and deploying robust applications.

Benefits of Microservices: Agility, Scalability, and Maintainability

In the fast-evolving landscape of software development, achieving agility, scalability, and maintainability is crucial for success. Microservices architecture, particularly when combined with serverless computing, offers a powerful approach to meeting these needs. This article explores the benefits of microservices, focusing on how they enhance agility, scalability, and maintainability. We will also discuss various design patterns for serverless applications and provide code examples to illustrate these concepts.

Agility

Faster Development and Deployment

Microservices architecture promotes agility by breaking down applications into smaller, independently deployable services. Each service encapsulates a specific business capability, allowing teams to develop, test, and deploy services independently. This modularity speeds up the development cycle and enables continuous delivery of new features.

```python
# Example AWS Lambda function for a User Service
import json
import boto3

dynamodb = boto3.resource('dynamodb')
table = dynamodb.Table('Users')

def lambda_handler(event, context):
    user_id = event['pathParameters']['id']
    response = table.get_item(Key={'user_id': user_id})
    if 'Item' in response:
        return {
            'statusCode': 200,
            'body': json.dumps(response['Item'])
        }
```

```
    else:
        return {
            'statusCode': 404,
            'body': json.dumps({'error': 'User not found'})
        }
```

Independent Development Teams

Microservices enable the division of development work among small, cross-functional teams. Each team can focus on a specific service, fostering ownership and accountability. This approach enhances collaboration and accelerates development by allowing teams to work concurrently without interfering with each other.

Continuous Integration and Continuous Deployment (CI/CD)

Microservices architecture aligns well with CI/CD practices. Automated pipelines can be set up for each service, ensuring that changes are tested and deployed rapidly. This continuous feedback loop helps teams respond quickly to changing requirements and improves overall software quality.

```yaml
```

```
# Example CI/CD pipeline configuration for a serverless application (GitHub Actions)
name: Deploy User Service
on:
  push:
    branches:
      - main
jobs:
  deploy:
    runs-on: ubuntu-latest
    steps:
      - name: Checkout code
        uses: actions/checkout@v2
      - name: Install Serverless Framework
        run: npm install -g serverless
      - name: Deploy to AWS
        run: sls deploy -v
        env:
```

```
      AWS_ACCESS_KEY_ID: ${{
secrets.AWS_ACCESS_KEY_ID }}

      AWS_SECRET_ACCESS_KEY: ${{
secrets.AWS_SECRET_ACCESS_KEY }}
```

Scalability

Automatic Scaling

One of the standout benefits of microservices, especially in a serverless context, is automatic scaling. Serverless platforms like AWS Lambda automatically scale functions in response to demand. This ensures that your application can handle varying loads without manual intervention, providing both cost efficiency and reliability.

```python
# Example AWS Lambda function with automatic scaling

import json

def lambda_handler(event, context):
    # Simulate processing based on input data
    data = json.loads(event['body'])
    processed_data = process_data(data)
```

```
    return {
        'statusCode': 200,
        'body': json.dumps(processed_data)
    }
def process_data(data):
    # Business logic to process data
    return {"processed": data}
```

Resource Efficiency

Serverless microservices only consume resources when they are actively processing requests. This pay-per-use model ensures that you are not paying for idle resources, optimizing costs and making your infrastructure more efficient.

Load Balancing and Distribution

Microservices can be deployed across multiple instances and regions, distributing the load evenly and enhancing fault tolerance. Load balancers can route traffic to the healthiest instances, ensuring high availability and performance.

```yaml
```

```yaml
# Example AWS API Gateway configuration with load balancing
service: my-microservices

provider:
  name: aws
  runtime: python3.8

functions:
  processRequest:
    handler: handler.lambda_handler
    events:
      - http:
          path: process
          method: post

resources:
  Resources:
    ApiGatewayRestApi:
      Type: 'AWS::ApiGateway::RestApi'
      Properties:
```

        Name: 'MyMicroservicesAPI'

        MinimumCompressionSize: 1024

```

## Maintainability

### Modular Codebase

Microservices architecture promotes a modular codebase, where each service is a self-contained unit. This separation makes the codebase easier to understand, maintain, and refactor. Changes in one service do not affect others, reducing the risk of introducing bugs and making the system more resilient.

```python
# Example AWS Lambda function for an Order Service

import json

import boto3

dynamodb = boto3.resource('dynamodb')

table = dynamodb.Table('Orders')

def lambda_handler(event, context):
    order_id = event['pathParameters']['id']

    response = table.get_item(Key={'order_id': order_id})
```
```

```
    if 'Item' in response:

        return {

            'statusCode': 200,

            'body': json.dumps(response['Item'])

        }

    else:

        return {

            'statusCode': 404,

            'body': json.dumps({'error': 'Order not found'})

        }
```

Simplified Testing

The independence of microservices simplifies testing. Each service can be tested in isolation, allowing for more focused and efficient testing strategies. Unit tests, integration tests, and end-to-end tests can be tailored to each service's specific requirements.

Clear Service Boundaries

Microservices enforce clear service boundaries, making it easier to define and manage the responsibilities of each service. This clarity helps in maintaining a clean architecture, where each service has a well-defined purpose and interacts with other services through standardized APIs.

```json
# Example OpenAPI Specification for a microservice

{
  "openapi": "3.0.0",
  "info": {
    "title": "User Service API",
    "version": "1.0.0"
  },
  "paths": {
    "/users/{id}": {
      "get": {
        "summary": "Get user by ID",
        "parameters": [
          {
            "name": "id",
```

```json
          "in": "path",
          "required": true,
          "schema": {
            "type": "string"
          }
      "responses": {
        "200": {
          "description": "User found",
          "content": {
            "application/json": {
              "schema": {
                "$ref": "#/components/schemas/User"
        },
        "404": {
          "description": "User not found"
  },
  "components": {
```

```
    "schemas": {
      "User": {
        "type": "object",
        "properties": {
          "user_id": {
            "type": "string"
          },
          "name": {
            "type": "string"
          },
          "email": {
            "type": "string"
          }
}
```

Event-Driven Architecture

Event-driven architecture is a key pattern in microservices that enhances maintainability by decoupling services. Events trigger actions in other services, allowing them to operate independently and reducing dependencies.

```python
# Example AWS Lambda function triggered by SNS
import json
import boto3

sns = boto3.client('sns')

def lambda_handler(event, context):
    message = {
        "event": "order_created",
        "order_id": "12345"
    }
    sns.publish(
        TopicArn='arn:aws:sns:us-east-1:123456789012:OrderEvents',
        Message=json.dumps(message)
    )
```

Saga Pattern

The Saga pattern is used to manage complex transactions across multiple microservices. Each service performs a local transaction and publishes an event to trigger the next step. If a step fails, compensating transactions are executed to maintain consistency.

```json
{
  "Comment": "Order processing saga",
  "StartAt": "CreateOrder",
  "States": {
    "CreateOrder": {
      "Type": "Task",
      "Resource": "arn:aws:lambda:us-east-1:123456789012:function:CreateOrder",
      "Next": "ReserveInventory"
    },
    "ReserveInventory": {
      "Type": "Task",
```

```
    "Resource": "arn:aws:lambda:us-east-1:123456789012:function:ReserveInventory",

    "Next": "ProcessPayment"

},

"ProcessPayment": {

    "Type": "Task",

    "Resource": "arn:aws:lambda:us-east-1:123456789012:function:ProcessPayment",

    "End": true

}
```

Microservices architecture, especially when combined with serverless computing, offers significant benefits in terms of agility, scalability, and maintainability. By breaking down applications into smaller, independent services, organizations can accelerate development cycles, scale efficiently, and maintain a clean and modular codebase.

Agility is achieved through faster development and deployment cycles, independent team structures, and robust CI/CD pipelines. Scalability is enhanced by automatic scaling, efficient resource utilization, and load balancing. Maintainability is improved through modular codebases, simplified testing, clear service boundaries, and event-driven architectures.

By leveraging design patterns such as FaaS, API Gateway, decentralized data management, event-driven architecture, Saga, Circuit Breaker, and Fan-out/Fan-in, developers can build robust, scalable, and maintainable serverless applications. This powerful combination not only addresses the challenges of modern software development but also positions organizations to respond quickly to changing market demands and technological advancements.

Challenges of Microservices: Communication, Complexity, and Testing

Microservices architecture has become increasingly popular due to its numerous benefits, including agility, scalability, and maintainability. However, it also introduces significant challenges, particularly in the areas of communication, complexity, and testing. When combined with serverless computing, these challenges can become even more pronounced. This article explores these challenges in depth, providing insights and code examples to illustrate how they can be managed effectively using microservices design patterns for serverless applications.

Communication

Inter-Service Communication

In a microservices architecture, each service operates independently, often running on different servers or even different cloud environments. This independence necessitates robust mechanisms for inter-service communication. Common protocols include HTTP/REST, gRPC, and messaging systems such as AWS SQS (Simple Queue Service) or SNS (Simple Notification Service).

- **Challenge**: Ensuring reliable and efficient communication between services, handling failures, and maintaining data consistency.
- **Solution**: Using API Gateway and messaging patterns.

```yaml
# Example AWS API Gateway configuration for serverless (serverless.yml)

service: user-service

provider:
  name: aws
  runtime: python3.8

functions:
  getUser:
    handler: handler.lambda_handler
```

```
events:
  - http:
      path: users/{id}
      method: get
```

Asynchronous Communication

Asynchronous communication can help decouple services and improve resilience. Messaging systems like AWS SNS/SQS allow services to publish and consume messages without blocking.

```python
# Example AWS Lambda function triggered by SNS
import json
import boto3

sns = boto3.client('sns')

def lambda_handler(event, context):
    message = {
        "event": "user_created",
        "user_id": "12345"
```

```
    }

    sns.publish(
        TopicArn='arn:aws:sns:us-east-1:123456789012:UserEvents',
        Message=json.dumps(message)
    )
```

Circuit Breaker Pattern

The Circuit Breaker pattern helps prevent cascading failures by monitoring service interactions and stopping requests to a failing service.

```python
# Example Circuit Breaker implementation in a Lambda function
import requests
from requests.exceptions import HTTPError

def lambda_handler(event, context):
    url = "https://example.com/api/resource"
    try:
```

```
        response = requests.get(url)

        response.raise_for_status()

        return response.json()

    except HTTPError as http_err:

        print(f"HTTP error occurred: {http_err}")

        raise

    except Exception as err:

        print(f"Other error occurred: {err}")

        raise
```

Complexity

Service Discovery

In a dynamic environment where services may be added, removed, or relocated frequently, service discovery mechanisms are essential. Service discovery allows services to find each other dynamically.

- **Challenge**: Managing the dynamic nature of microservices, ensuring they can discover and communicate with each other reliably.
- **Solution**: Using service discovery tools like AWS Cloud Map or Consul.

Data Management

Microservices promote decentralized data management, where each service owns its own database. This approach can lead to data consistency issues.

- **Challenge**: Ensuring data consistency across multiple services.
- **Solution**: Using the Saga pattern for managing distributed transactions.

```json
{
  "Comment": "Order processing saga",
  "StartAt": "CreateOrder",
  "States": {
    "CreateOrder": {
      "Type": "Task",
      "Resource": "arn:aws:lambda:us-east-1:123456789012:function:CreateOrder",
      "Next": "ReserveInventory"
    },
    "ReserveInventory": {
```

```
    "Type": "Task",

    "Resource": "arn:aws:lambda:us-east-1:123456789012:function:ReserveInventory",

    "Next": "ProcessPayment"

},

"ProcessPayment": {

    "Type": "Task",

    "Resource": "arn:aws:lambda:us-east-1:123456789012:function:ProcessPayment",

    "End": true

}
```

Dependency Management

Managing dependencies between services can be challenging, especially as the number of services grows.

- **Challenge**: Handling interdependencies without causing tight coupling.
- **Solution**: Implementing API Gateway for centralized management and employing the Fan-out/Fan-in pattern.

```python
```

```python
# Example Fan-out with AWS Lambda and SNS
import json
import boto3
sns = boto3.client('sns')
def lambda_handler(event, context):
    message = {"task": "process_data"}
    sns.publish(
        TopicArn='arn:aws:sns:us-east-1:123456789012:DataProcessing',
        Message=json.dumps(message)
    )
# Example Fan-in with AWS Lambda and SQS
def lambda_handler(event, context):
    for record in event['Records']:
        message_body = json.loads(record['body'])
        process_message(message_body)
def process_message(message):
    print(f"Processing message: {message}")
```

```
# Business logic here
```

Testing

Unit Testing

Unit testing in a microservices architecture requires testing each service in isolation. However, due to the nature of microservices, dependencies between services need to be mocked or simulated.

- **Challenge**: Creating isolated environments for each service to test their functionalities without external dependencies.
- **Solution**: Using mocking frameworks and dependency injection.

```python
# Example unit test for a Lambda function using unittest and moto for AWS mocks

import unittest

from moto import mock_dynamodb2

import boto3

import json

@mock_dynamodb2
```

```python
class TestUserService(unittest.TestCase):
    def setUp(self):
        self.dynamodb = boto3.resource('dynamodb', region_name='us-east-1')
        self.table = self.dynamodb.create_table(
            TableName='Users',
            KeySchema=[{'AttributeName': 'user_id', 'KeyType': 'HASH'}],
            AttributeDefinitions=[{'AttributeName': 'user_id', 'AttributeType': 'S'}],
            ProvisionedThroughput={'ReadCapacityUnits': 1, 'WriteCapacityUnits': 1}
        )
        self.table.put_item(Item={'user_id': '12345', 'name': 'John Doe', 'email': 'john@example.com'})

    def test_get_user(self):
        from handler import lambda_handler
        event = {'pathParameters': {'id': '12345'}}
        response = lambda_handler(event, {})
        self.assertEqual(response['statusCode'], 200)
```

```
        self.assertIn('John Doe', response['body'])

if __name__ == '__main__':
    unittest.main()
```

Integration Testing

Integration testing ensures that services work together as expected. This involves setting up test environments that mimic production as closely as possible.

- **Challenge**: Coordinating multiple services for testing and managing test data across these services.
- **Solution**: Using tools like Docker Compose for local testing environments and AWS CloudFormation for cloud-based test environments.

```yaml
# Example Docker Compose configuration for local integration testing
version: '3.8'
services:
  user-service:
    image: user-service:latest
```

```
    ports:
      - "5000:5000"
    environment:
      - AWS_ACCESS_KEY_ID=mock
      - AWS_SECRET_ACCESS_KEY=mock
      - DYNAMODB_ENDPOINT=http://dynamodb:8000
  dynamodb:
    image: amazon/dynamodb-local
    ports:
      - "8000:8000"
```

End-to-End Testing

End-to-end (E2E) testing validates the entire application flow from start to finish. This type of testing simulates real user scenarios to ensure that all services work together correctly.

- **Challenge**: Creating comprehensive E2E tests that cover all critical paths and edge cases.
- **Solution**: Using frameworks like Selenium for web applications or Postman for API testing.

```json
// Example Postman collection for end-to-end testing
{
  "info": {
    "name": "Microservices E2E Tests",
    "schema": "https://schema.getpostman.com/json/collection/v2.1.0/collection.json"
  },
  "item": [
    {
      "name": "Create User",
      "request": {
        "method": "POST",
        "header": [
          {
            "key": "Content-Type",
            "value": "application/json"
```

```
      }
    "body": {
      "mode": "raw",
      "raw": "{\"user_id\": \"12345\", \"name\": \"John Doe\", \"email\": \"john@example.com\"}"
    },
    "url": {
      "raw": "http://localhost:5000/users",
      "protocol": "http",
      "host": [
        "localhost"
      ],
      "port": "5000",
      "path": [
        "users"
      ]
  },
  "response": []
},
```

```
    "name": "Get User",
    "request": {
      "method": "GET",
      "url": {
        "raw": "http://localhost:5000/users/12345",
        "protocol": "http",
        "host": [
          "localhost"
        ],
        "port": "5000",
        "path": [
          "users",
          "12345"
        ]
      },
      "response": []
  }
```

Microservices architecture, while offering numerous benefits such as agility, scalability, and maintainability, also introduces significant challenges in communication, complexity, and testing. By employing design patterns and leveraging serverless technologies, these challenges can be effectively managed.

Communication challenges can be addressed using API Gateway, asynchronous messaging, and Circuit Breaker patterns. Complexity can be managed through service discovery, Saga pattern for distributed transactions, and dependency management with Fan-out/Fan-in patterns.

Designing Effective Microservices: Best Practices and Considerations

Microservices architecture has become increasingly popular for building scalable and resilient applications, especially in the realm of serverless computing. By decomposing applications into small, independent services, microservices enable agility, scalability, and fault tolerance. However, designing effective microservices for serverless applications requires careful consideration of various factors, including architecture, communication patterns, data management, and deployment strategies. In this article, we'll explore best practices and considerations for designing microservices for serverless applications, with a focus on incorporating microservices design patterns and code examples.

1. Define Clear Service Boundaries:

Clear service boundaries are crucial in microservices architecture to ensure each service has a single responsibility and encapsulates a specific business capability. Let's consider an example of an e-commerce application:

```python
# User Service

@app.route('/users', methods=['GET'])

def get_users():

    # Logic to retrieve users from database

    pass

@app.route('/users/<user_id>', methods=['GET'])

def get_user(user_id):

    # Logic to retrieve a user by ID from database

    pass
```

2. Choose the Right Data Storage Strategy:

When designing microservices for serverless applications, consider using serverless data storage solutions like AWS DynamoDB for scalable and low-latency access to data.

```python
import boto3

# Initialize DynamoDB client
dynamodb = boto3.client('dynamodb')

# Example of retrieving data from DynamoDB
response = dynamodb.get_item(
    TableName='UserTable',
    Key={
        'userId': {'S': '123'}
    }
```

3. Embrace Asynchronous Communication:

Asynchronous communication between microservices helps decouple services and improve resilience. Utilize messaging services like AWS SQS for event-driven communication.

```python
import boto3

# Initialize SQS client
```

```
sqs = boto3.client('sqs')

# Send message to SQS queue

response = sqs.send_message(
    QueueUrl='QUEUE_URL',
    MessageBody='{"user_id": "123", "event": "login"}'
)
```

4. Implement Circuit Breaker and Retry Mechanisms:

Implement circuit breaker and retry mechanisms to handle failures gracefully and prevent cascading failures.

```python
from circuitbreaker import CircuitBreaker

# Example of using a circuit breaker

@CircuitBreaker
def call_microservice():
    # Logic to call microservice
    pass
```

```

## 5. Monitor and Trace Service Interactions:

Implement logging, monitoring, and distributed tracing solutions to monitor service interactions and diagnose issues.

```python

import logging

# Configure logging

logging.basicConfig(level=logging.INFO)

# Example of logging

logging.info('User logged in')

```

6. Automate Deployment and Infrastructure Provisioning:

Automate deployment and infrastructure provisioning using tools like AWS CloudFormation or Serverless Framework.

```yaml

# Example AWS SAM template for deploying Lambda function

```
Resources:
  MyFunction:
    Type: AWS::Serverless::Function
    Properties:
      Handler: index.handler
      Runtime: python3.8
```

7. Design for Scalability and Resilience:

Design microservices to be stateless and horizontally scalable to handle fluctuations in workload.

```python
# Example of stateless microservice using AWS Lambda
def lambda_handler(event, context):
    # Handle request
    pass
```

8. Implement Security Best Practices:

Implement security best practices such as least privilege access, encryption, and secure communication protocols.

```python
# Example of using AWS IAM for access control
import boto3
# Initialize IAM client
iam = boto3.client('iam')
# Example of creating IAM policy
response = iam.create_policy(
    PolicyName='MyPolicy',
    PolicyDocument={
        'Version': '2012-10-17',
        'Statement': [{
            'Effect': 'Allow',
            'Action': 's3:*',
            'Resource': '*'
        }
```

Designing effective microservices for serverless applications involves careful consideration of architecture, communication patterns, data management, and deployment strategies. By following best practices such as defining clear service boundaries, choosing the right data storage strategy, embracing asynchronous communication, implementing resilience patterns, monitoring and tracing service interactions, automating deployment and infrastructure provisioning, designing for scalability and resilience, and implementing security best practices, teams can build scalable, resilient, and secure serverless applications using microservices architecture. By leveraging microservices design patterns and incorporating code examples, organizations can create robust and efficient serverless applications that meet the demands of modern cloud computing environments.

Chapter 3

Introduction to Serverless Computing: A Pay-as-You-Go Revolution

What is Serverless Computing? Shifting Focus to Code, not Infrastructure

Serverless computing, also known as Function as a Service (FaaS), is a cloud computing paradigm that abstracts away server management, allowing developers to focus solely on writing and deploying code. In serverless computing, developers upload functions to a cloud provider, which takes care of provisioning, scaling, and managing the underlying infrastructure. This paradigm shift enables developers to build and deploy applications more quickly, efficiently, and cost-effectively. In this article, we'll explore what serverless computing is, its benefits, and how it aligns with microservices design patterns, accompanied by code examples.

Understanding Serverless Computing:

Serverless computing abstracts away the complexity of infrastructure management, allowing developers to write code without worrying about servers, scaling, or maintenance. Instead of provisioning and managing servers, developers focus on writing functions that perform specific tasks or operations. These functions are triggered by events, such as HTTP requests, database updates, or scheduled events, and are executed in response to these events. Serverless platforms automatically scale the infrastructure based on demand, ensuring that applications remain responsive and cost-effective.

Benefits of Serverless Computing:

1. Scalability: Serverless platforms automatically scale resources up or down based on workload, ensuring optimal performance and responsiveness.

2. Cost-Effectiveness: With serverless computing, developers only pay for the resources consumed by their functions, eliminating the need to provision and maintain costly infrastructure.

3. Simplicity: Serverless computing abstracts away infrastructure management, allowing developers to focus solely on writing and deploying code, thereby reducing complexity and speeding up development cycles.

4. Flexibility: Serverless platforms support a wide range of programming languages and frameworks, giving developers the flexibility to choose the tools that best suit their needs.

5. Resilience: Serverless architectures are inherently resilient, with built-in fault tolerance and redundancy at the infrastructure level.

Microservices Design Patterns for Serverless Applications:

Serverless computing aligns well with microservices architecture, a design approach where applications are composed of small, independent services that communicate through APIs. Microservices promote modularity, scalability, and flexibility, making them an ideal fit for serverless applications. Here are some microservices design patterns commonly used in serverless applications, accompanied by code examples:

1. Stateless Functions:

Serverless functions are typically stateless, meaning they don't maintain any internal state between invocations. This enables easy scaling and fault tolerance.

```python
# Example of a stateless function in Python using AWS Lambda

def lambda_handler(event, context):
    # Handle request
    return {
        'statusCode': 200,
        'body': 'Hello, World!'
    }
```

2. Event-Driven Architecture:

Serverless applications are often designed around event-driven architecture, where functions are triggered by events such as HTTP requests, database changes, or file uploads.

```python
# Example of an event-driven function triggered by an HTTP request

@app.route('/hello', methods=['GET'])

def hello():

    return 'Hello, World!'
```

3. Asynchronous Communication:

Microservices in serverless applications communicate asynchronously using messaging services like AWS SQS or SNS, decoupling services and improving scalability and resilience.

```python
# Example of sending a message to an SQS queue

import boto3

# Initialize SQS client
```

```python
sqs = boto3.client('sqs')

# Send message to SQS queue
response = sqs.send_message(
    QueueUrl='QUEUE_URL',
    MessageBody='{"user_id": "123", "event": "login"}'
)
```

4. API Gateway Integration:

Serverless functions can be exposed as APIs using API Gateway, allowing them to be accessed over HTTP.

```python
# Example of integrating a Lambda function with API Gateway
import json

def lambda_handler(event, context):
    # Handle HTTP request
    return {
        'statusCode': 200,
```

```
        'body': json.dumps('Hello, World!')

    }
```

Serverless computing represents a paradigm shift in cloud computing, enabling developers to focus solely on writing and deploying code without worrying about infrastructure management. By abstracting away server management and scaling, serverless computing simplifies development, reduces costs, and accelerates time to market. When combined with microservices design patterns, serverless computing enables the creation of highly scalable, resilient, and flexible applications that can quickly adapt to changing business requirements. As organizations increasingly embrace cloud-native architectures, serverless computing and microservices will continue to play a central role in driving innovation and agility in the software development process.

Benefits of Serverless: Focus on Functionality, Automatic Scaling, and Cost Efficiency

Serverless computing has revolutionized the way developers build and deploy applications, offering a range of benefits that improve agility, scalability, and cost-effectiveness. By abstracting away server management and infrastructure provisioning, serverless computing enables developers to focus solely on writing code to deliver business functionality. In this article, we'll delve into the benefits of serverless, with a focus on functionality, automatic scaling, and cost efficiency, accompanied by code examples based on microservices design patterns for serverless applications.

1. Focus on Functionality:

Serverless computing allows developers to focus exclusively on writing code to implement business functionality, without the overhead of managing servers or infrastructure. This enables teams to accelerate development cycles and deliver features to market more quickly. With serverless platforms handling infrastructure provisioning, scaling, and maintenance, developers can devote more time and resources to building and improving application functionality.

Example:

```python
# Example of a serverless function implementing business logic

def calculate_order_total(order):
    total = 0
    for item in order['items']:
        total += item['price'] * item['quantity']
    return total
```

```

## 2. Automatic Scaling:

Serverless platforms automatically scale resources up or down based on demand, ensuring optimal performance and responsiveness without manual intervention. This elasticity enables applications to handle spikes in traffic or workload without experiencing downtime or performance degradation. By dynamically allocating resources as needed, serverless platforms minimize idle capacity and optimize resource utilization, resulting in cost savings and improved efficiency.

**Example**:

```python
# Example of a serverless function automatically scaling to handle increased traffic

@app.route('/process_order', methods=['POST'])

def process_order():

    # Process order logic

    return 'Order processed successfully'
```

3. Cost Efficiency:
```

Serverless computing offers cost efficiency by charging only for the resources consumed by functions, rather than provisioning and maintaining fixed infrastructure. With serverless platforms, organizations pay only for the compute time, memory, and other resources used during function execution, eliminating the need for upfront investments in hardware or provisioning of idle capacity. This pay-as-you-go pricing model enables organizations to align costs with actual usage and scale resources cost-effectively as demand fluctuates.

Example:

```python

# Example of calculating cost savings with serverless computing

total_cost = function_execution_time * memory_allocated * price_per_execution

```

Microservices Design Patterns for Serverless Applications:

Serverless computing aligns well with microservices architecture, a design approach where applications are composed of small, independent services that communicate through APIs. Microservices promote modularity, scalability, and flexibility, making them an ideal fit for serverless applications. Here's how microservices design patterns enhance the benefits of serverless:

1. Stateless Functions:

Serverless functions are typically stateless, meaning they don't maintain any internal state between invocations. This simplifies scaling and ensures resilience and fault tolerance.

Example:

```python
# Example of a stateless function in Python using AWS Lambda

def lambda_handler(event, context):
    # Handle request
    return {
        'statusCode': 200,
        'body': 'Hello, World!'
    }
```

2. Event-Driven Architecture:

Serverless applications are often designed around event-driven architecture, where functions are triggered by events such as HTTP requests, database changes, or file uploads. This promotes loose coupling and allows services to react dynamically to changes in the environment.

Example:

```python
# Example of an event-driven function triggered by an HTTP request

@app.route('/hello', methods=['GET'])

def hello():

    return 'Hello, World!'
```

3. Asynchronous Communication:

Microservices in serverless applications communicate asynchronously using messaging services like AWS SQS or SNS, decoupling services and improving scalability and resilience.

Example:

```python
# Example of sending a message to an SQS queue
```

```
import boto3

# Initialize SQS client

sqs = boto3.client('sqs')

# Send message to SQS queue

response = sqs.send_message(
    QueueUrl='QUEUE_URL',
    MessageBody='{"user_id": "123", "event": "login"}'
)
```
```

Serverless computing offers a range of benefits, including a focus on functionality, automatic scaling, and cost efficiency. By abstracting away server management and infrastructure provisioning, serverless platforms enable developers to concentrate on building and delivering business value. When combined with microservices design patterns, serverless computing enables the creation of highly scalable, resilient, and cost-effective applications that can quickly adapt to changing business requirements. As organizations continue to embrace cloud-native architectures, serverless computing and microservices will play an increasingly pivotal role in driving innovation and agility in the software development process.
```

How Does Serverless Work? Events, Triggers, and Functions in Action

Serverless computing has become increasingly popular for building scalable and efficient applications in the cloud. But how does serverless actually work? In this article, we'll explore the inner workings of serverless computing, focusing on events, triggers, and functions, and how they come together to create dynamic and responsive applications. We'll also provide code examples based on microservices design patterns for serverless applications to illustrate these concepts in action.

1. Understanding Serverless Architecture:

At its core, serverless computing abstracts away the management of servers and infrastructure, allowing developers to focus solely on writing code to implement business logic. In a serverless architecture, applications are composed of small, independent functions that are executed in response to events or triggers. These functions are stateless and ephemeral, meaning they don't maintain any internal state between invocations and can be dynamically provisioned and scaled based on demand.

2. Events and Triggers:

Events and triggers are central to serverless computing, as they determine when functions are executed. An event is a change in the system's state or an occurrence that triggers the execution of a function. Triggers are mechanisms that detect these events and invoke the corresponding function. Common types of events and triggers in serverless applications include HTTP requests, database changes, file uploads, scheduled events, and message queue notifications.

3. Functions:

Functions are the building blocks of serverless applications. A function is a small piece of code that performs a specific task or operation in response to an event. Functions are stateless and can be written in a variety of programming languages, such as Python, JavaScript, Java, or C#. Serverless platforms, such as AWS Lambda, Azure Functions, or Google Cloud Functions, execute functions in ephemeral containers or virtual machines, dynamically allocating resources based on demand.

4. Example: Handling HTTP Requests with Serverless Functions:

Let's consider an example of handling HTTP requests using serverless functions. In this scenario, we have a microservice architecture where each function corresponds to a specific endpoint in our application.

```python

# Example of an HTTP trigger function in Python using AWS Lambda

def lambda_handler(event, context):
```

```python
# Extract request parameters from event
http_method = event['httpMethod']
path = event['path']
query_params = event['queryStringParameters']
body = event['body']
# Perform business logic based on request
if http_method == 'GET' and path == '/users':
    # Retrieve list of users from database
    return {
        'statusCode': 200,
        'body': json.dumps(users)
    }
elif http_method == 'POST' and path == '/users':
    # Create a new user
    user_data = json.loads(body)
    # Insert user data into database
    return {
```

```
            'statusCode': 201,

            'body': json.dumps('User created successfully')

        }

    else:

        return {

            'statusCode': 404,

            'body': json.dumps('Not found')

        }
```

In this example, the `lambda_handler` function is triggered by HTTP requests received by API Gateway, a managed service provided by AWS. The function extracts request parameters from the event object and performs business logic based on the HTTP method and path. The function then returns an appropriate HTTP response based on the outcome of the business logic.

5. Benefits of Serverless Architecture:

Serverless architecture offers several benefits, including:

- **Scalability**: Serverless platforms automatically scale resources up or down based on demand, ensuring optimal performance and responsiveness.

- **Cost Efficiency:** With serverless computing, organizations only pay for the resources consumed by functions, eliminating the need to provision and maintain costly infrastructure.
- **Simplicity**: Serverless computing abstracts away infrastructure management, allowing developers to focus solely on writing and deploying code, thereby reducing complexity and speeding up development cycles.
- **Flexibility**: Serverless platforms support a wide range of programming languages and frameworks, giving developers the flexibility to choose the tools that best suit their needs.

Serverless computing operates on the principles of events, triggers, and functions, enabling developers to build dynamic and responsive applications without worrying about server management or infrastructure provisioning. By leveraging microservices design patterns, organizations can create highly scalable, efficient, and cost-effective applications that can quickly adapt to changing business requirements. As organizations continue to embrace cloud-native architectures, serverless computing will play an increasingly critical role in driving innovation and agility in the software development process.

Key Features of Serverless Platforms (e.g., AWS Lambda, Azure Functions)

Serverless computing platforms, such as AWS Lambda and Azure Functions, offer a range of features that enable developers to build scalable, efficient, and cost-effective applications. In this article, we'll explore the key features of AWS Lambda and Azure Functions, with a focus on how they support microservices design patterns for serverless applications. We'll also provide code examples to illustrate these features in action.

1. Event-Driven Architecture:

Serverless platforms are built around event-driven architecture, where functions are triggered by events such as HTTP requests, database changes, file uploads, or scheduled events. AWS Lambda and Azure Functions support a wide range of event sources, allowing developers to react dynamically to changes in the environment.

Example:

```python
# AWS Lambda function triggered by an S3 upload event

import boto3

s3 = boto3.client('s3')

def lambda_handler(event, context):
    for record in event['Records']:
        bucket = record['s3']['bucket']['name']
```

```
    key = record['s3']['object']['key']

    # Process uploaded file

    print(f'File uploaded: s3://{bucket}/{key}')
```

2. Scalability:

AWS Lambda and Azure Functions automatically scale resources up or down based on demand, ensuring optimal performance and responsiveness without manual intervention. Functions are executed in ephemeral containers or virtual machines, dynamically allocating resources based on workload.

Example:

```python
# Azure Function triggered by an HTTP request

import azure.functions as func

def main(req: func.HttpRequest) -> func.HttpResponse:
    return func.HttpResponse("Hello, World!")
```

3. Pay-Per-Use Pricing:

Serverless platforms offer a pay-per-use pricing model, where organizations only pay for the resources consumed by functions, eliminating the need to provision and maintain costly infrastructure. This pricing model allows organizations to align costs with actual usage and scale resources cost-effectively as demand fluctuates.

Example:

```python

# AWS Lambda function calculating cost savings

total_cost = function_execution_time * memory_allocated * price_per_execution

```

4. Built-In Integrations:

AWS Lambda and Azure Functions provide built-in integrations with other cloud services, allowing developers to easily connect functions to event sources, databases, messaging services, and more. These integrations streamline development and enable seamless communication between components of serverless applications.

Example:

```python

# AWS Lambda function triggered by an SQS message
```

```
import boto3

sqs = boto3.client('sqs')

def lambda_handler(event, context):
    for record in event['Records']:
        # Process message from SQS queue
        print(record['body'])
```

5. Language and Runtime Support:

AWS Lambda and Azure Functions support a wide range of programming languages and frameworks, giving developers the flexibility to choose the tools that best suit their needs. Supported languages include Python, JavaScript, Java, C#, and more.

Example:

```python
# AWS Lambda function written in Python
def lambda_handler(event, context):
    # Handle request
    return {
```

```
    'statusCode': 200,
    'body': 'Hello, World!'
}
```

6. Security and Compliance:

Serverless platforms provide built-in security features, such as access control, encryption, and monitoring, to ensure the confidentiality, integrity, and availability of applications and data. AWS Lambda and Azure Functions integrate with cloud-native security services, such as AWS IAM and Azure Active Directory, to enforce least privilege access and secure communication between components.

Example:

```python
# AWS Lambda function with IAM permissions
import boto3

s3 = boto3.client('s3')

def lambda_handler(event, context):
    # Perform operations with restricted IAM permissions
    s3.list_buckets()
```

```

AWS Lambda and Azure Functions offer a range of features that enable developers to build scalable, efficient, and cost-effective serverless applications. By leveraging event-driven architecture, scalability, pay-per-use pricing, built-in integrations, language and runtime support, and security and compliance features, organizations can create highly responsive, flexible, and secure applications that can quickly adapt to changing business requirements. As organizations continue to adopt cloud-native architectures, serverless computing will play an increasingly critical role in driving innovation and agility in the software development process.
```

Chapter 4

Choosing the Right Programming Languages for Serverless Functions

Selecting the appropriate programming language for serverless functions is crucial for the success of your serverless applications. Each language has its strengths and weaknesses, and choosing the right one can impact factors such as development speed, performance, scalability, and maintainability. In this article, we'll explore the factors to consider when choosing programming languages for serverless functions and provide examples based on microservices design patterns for serverless applications.

1. Performance:

Performance is a critical factor to consider when choosing a programming language for serverless functions. Some languages may offer better performance for specific use cases or workloads. For example, languages like C++ or Rust may offer better performance for CPU-intensive tasks, while languages like Node.js or Python may be better suited for I/O-bound tasks.

Example:

```javascript
// Node.js function for processing I/O-bound tasks
```

```
exports.handler = async (event) => {

    // Process I/O-bound tasks

    return 'Task completed';

};
```

2. Development Speed:

Development speed is another important consideration, especially in agile development environments where time-to-market is critical. Languages with concise syntax and robust libraries can accelerate the development process and reduce the time and effort required to implement serverless functions.

Example:

```python
# Python function for processing data using concise syntax

def lambda_handler(event, context):

    # Process data

    return 'Data processed successfully'
```

3. Community Support and Ecosystem:

Community support and ecosystem play a significant role in the success of a programming language for serverless functions. Languages with large and active communities often have extensive libraries, frameworks, and tools that can streamline development and provide solutions to common challenges.

Example:

```javascript
// JavaScript function with access to a rich ecosystem of libraries and frameworks

exports.handler = async (event) => {

    // Use third-party libraries and frameworks

    return 'Task completed';

};
```

4. Integration with Serverless Platforms:

Some programming languages may have better integration with specific serverless platforms, offering features or capabilities that are optimized for that platform. For example, AWS Lambda has first-class support for Node.js and Python, while Azure Functions offers seamless integration with .NET languages like C#.

Example:

```csharp
// C# function for processing data with Azure Functions
using Microsoft.Azure.Functions.Worker;
using Microsoft.Extensions.Logging;
public class Function1
{
    [Function("Function1")]
    public static string Run([QueueTrigger("myqueue-items", Connection = "AzureWebJobsStorage")] string myQueueItem, FunctionContext context)
    {
        var logger = context.GetLogger("Function1");
        logger.LogInformation($"C# Queue trigger function processed: {myQueueItem}");
        return myQueueItem;
    }
}
```

5. Language Familiarity and Team Skills:

The familiarity and skill level of your development team with a particular programming language can also influence the choice of language for serverless functions. Choosing a language that your team is comfortable with can improve productivity and reduce the learning curve.

Example:

```typescript
// TypeScript function for processing data, suitable for teams familiar with JavaScript

export async function handler(event: any): Promise<any> {

    // Process data

    return 'Data processed successfully';

}
```

Choosing the right programming language for serverless functions requires careful consideration of factors such as performance, development speed, community support, integration with serverless platforms, and team skills. By evaluating these factors and selecting a language that aligns with your project requirements and objectives, you can ensure the success of your serverless applications. Whether you choose Node.js, Python, Java, C#, or another language, leveraging microservices design patterns for serverless applications can help you build scalable, efficient, and maintainable applications that meet the demands of modern cloud computing environments.

Serverless Frameworks: Simplifying Development and Deployment (e.g., Serverless Framework, AWS SAM)

Serverless frameworks have become essential tools for developers building serverless applications, offering features and abstractions that simplify development, deployment, and management. In this article, we'll explore popular serverless frameworks like Serverless Framework and AWS SAM (Serverless Application Model), and discuss how they streamline the development and deployment of serverless applications. We'll also provide code examples based on microservices design patterns for serverless applications to illustrate the usage of these frameworks.

1. Serverless Framework:

Serverless Framework is an open-source framework that provides developers with a set of tools and abstractions for building serverless applications. It supports multiple cloud providers, including AWS, Azure, Google Cloud Platform, and more, allowing developers to write serverless functions using familiar languages like Node.js, Python, Java, and C#. Serverless Framework abstracts away the complexity of infrastructure management, enabling developers to focus solely on writing code to implement business logic.

Features of Serverless Framework:

- **Declarative Configuration:** Serverless Framework allows developers to define the configuration of their serverless applications using a declarative YAML file, making it easy to manage and maintain infrastructure as code.
- **Built-In Deployment:** Serverless Framework provides built-in deployment capabilities that automate the provisioning of resources and the deployment of serverless functions to the cloud provider.
- **Plugin System:** Serverless Framework offers a rich ecosystem of plugins that extend its functionality and enable integration with third-party services, libraries, and tools.

Example:

```yaml
# serverless.yml - Example configuration for Serverless Framework

service: my-service

provider:
  name: aws
```

```
    runtime: nodejs14.x

  functions:

    hello:

      handler: handler.hello

      events:

        - http:

            path: hello

            method: get
```

2. AWS SAM (Serverless Application Model):

AWS SAM is an open-source framework provided by AWS for building serverless applications on AWS. It extends AWS CloudFormation to provide a simplified syntax for defining serverless resources, such as functions, APIs, and databases. AWS SAM makes it easy for developers to define, deploy, and manage serverless applications using AWS services like AWS Lambda, Amazon API Gateway, and Amazon DynamoDB.

Features of AWS SAM:

- **Simple Template Syntax:** AWS SAM introduces a simplified template syntax that

allows developers to define serverless resources using familiar constructs, such as AWS::Serverless::Function and AWS::Serverless::Api.
- **Local Testing and Debugging:** AWS SAM provides tools for testing and debugging serverless applications locally before deploying them to the cloud, enabling rapid iteration and development.
- **Built-In Integration with AWS Services:** AWS SAM integrates seamlessly with AWS services like AWS Lambda, Amazon API Gateway, and Amazon DynamoDB, making it easy to build serverless applications using these services.

Example:

```yaml
# template.yaml - Example AWS SAM template for defining a serverless function

Resources:
  HelloWorldFunction:
    Type: AWS::Serverless::Function
    Properties:
      Handler: hello.handler
      Runtime: nodejs14.x
```

```
  Events:
    HelloWorldApi:
      Type: Api
      Properties:
        Path: /hello
        Method: get
```

Microservices Design Patterns with Serverless Frameworks:

Serverless frameworks like Serverless Framework and AWS SAM are well-suited for implementing microservices architecture in serverless applications. They provide abstractions and tools that support microservices design patterns, such as event-driven architecture, loose coupling, and independent deployment.

Example:

```yaml
# serverless.yml - Example configuration for implementing microservices with Serverless Framework

service: my-service
```

```
provider:
  name: aws
  runtime: nodejs14.x
functions:
  user-service:
    handler: user.handler
    events:
      - http:
          path: users
          method: get
  order-service:
    handler: order.handler
    events:
      - http:
          path: orders
          method: get
```

Serverless frameworks like Serverless Framework and AWS SAM play a crucial role in simplifying the development and deployment of serverless applications. By providing abstractions, tools, and integrations with cloud providers, these frameworks enable developers to build scalable, efficient, and maintainable serverless applications using microservices design patterns. Whether you're building a small prototype or a large-scale production application, leveraging serverless frameworks can help you accelerate development, reduce operational overhead, and deliver better experiences for your users.

Integrating with APIs and Data Sources: Building the Microservices Ecosystem

Integrating with APIs and data sources is a crucial aspect of building a microservices ecosystem in serverless applications. Microservices often need to interact with external services, databases, and APIs to fulfill their functionality. In this article, we'll explore how to integrate serverless functions with APIs and data sources, leveraging microservices design patterns to build a scalable and efficient microservices ecosystem. We'll provide code examples to illustrate different integration scenarios and demonstrate best practices for building serverless applications.

1. Integrating with External APIs:

Serverless functions can interact with external APIs to fetch data, trigger actions, or integrate with third-party services. This allows microservices to extend their functionality beyond the confines of the application and leverage external resources to perform tasks.

Example:

```python
# Example of a serverless function integrating with an external API using Python and AWS Lambda

import requests

def lambda_handler(event, context):
    # Make a request to external API
    response = requests.get('https://api.example.com/data')
    data = response.json()
    # Process data
    return data
```

2. Integrating with Databases:

Microservices often need to store and retrieve data from databases to maintain state or persist information. Serverless applications can integrate with databases such as Amazon DynamoDB, MongoDB Atlas, or Google Cloud Firestore to store and query data efficiently.

Example:

```python
# Example of a serverless function integrating with a database using Python and AWS Lambda

import boto3

dynamodb = boto3.resource('dynamodb')

table = dynamodb.Table('my-table')

def lambda_handler(event, context):
    # Retrieve data from database
    response = table.get_item(Key={'id': '123'})
    item = response['Item']
    # Process data
    return item
```

3. Event-Driven Integration:

Microservices can integrate with other services using event-driven architecture, where events trigger the execution of serverless functions. This allows microservices to react to changes in the environment and perform actions asynchronously.

Example:

```python
# Example of an event-driven integration using AWS Lambda and S3
import boto3
s3 = boto3.client('s3')
def lambda_handler(event, context):
    # Process event triggered by S3 upload
    for record in event['Records']:
        bucket = record['s3']['bucket']['name']
        key = record['s3']['object']['key']
        # Process uploaded file
        print(f'File uploaded: s3://{bucket}/{key}')
```

4. API Gateway Integration:

Serverless functions can expose HTTP endpoints using API Gateway, allowing them to be accessed over the internet. This enables microservices to provide web APIs for interacting with external clients or services.

Example:

```python
# Example of an API Gateway integration using AWS Lambda and Python
import json

def lambda_handler(event, context):
    # Process HTTP request
    return {
        'statusCode': 200,
        'body': json.dumps('Hello, World!')
    }
```

5. Asynchronous Communication:

Microservices can communicate asynchronously using messaging services like Amazon SQS or AWS SNS. This decouples services and improves scalability, resilience, and fault tolerance.

Example:

```python
```

```
# Example of asynchronous communication using AWS Lambda and SQS

import boto3

sqs = boto3.client('sqs')

def lambda_handler(event, context):
    # Send message to SQS queue
    response = sqs.send_message(
        QueueUrl='QUEUE_URL',
        MessageBody='{"user_id": "123", "event": "login"}'
    )
    # Process response
    return response
```

Integrating serverless functions with APIs and data sources is essential for building a microservices ecosystem in serverless applications. By leveraging microservices design patterns and best practices, developers can build scalable, efficient, and maintainable serverless applications that interact seamlessly with external services and databases. Whether you're fetching data from external APIs, storing data in databases, reacting to events, exposing HTTP endpoints, or communicating asynchronously, serverless functions provide a flexible and powerful platform for building microservices that meet the demands of modern cloud-native architectures.

Monitoring and Debugging Tools for Serverless Applications (e.g., AWS CloudWatch)

Monitoring and debugging are critical aspects of maintaining and troubleshooting serverless applications. With the dynamic nature of serverless architectures, it's essential to have robust tools and practices in place to monitor performance, detect issues, and debug problems effectively. In this article, we'll explore monitoring and debugging tools for serverless applications, focusing on AWS CloudWatch as an example, and provide code examples based on microservices design patterns to illustrate how these tools can be used in practice.

1. AWS CloudWatch:

AWS CloudWatch is a monitoring and observability service provided by Amazon Web Services (AWS) for monitoring resources and applications running on AWS. It offers a range of features for monitoring serverless applications, including metrics, logs, alarms, and dashboards, to help developers gain insights into the performance and behavior of their applications.

Key Features of AWS CloudWatch:

- **Metrics**: AWS CloudWatch provides metrics for monitoring various aspects of serverless applications, such as function invocations, errors, durations, and resource utilization. These metrics can be used to track performance, identify bottlenecks, and optimize resource usage.
- **Logs**: AWS CloudWatch Logs allows developers to centralize and analyze logs generated by serverless functions and other AWS services. Logs can be searched, filtered, and monitored in real-time, making it easier to debug issues and troubleshoot problems.
- **Alarms**: AWS CloudWatch Alarms enable developers to set up notifications and triggers based on predefined thresholds or conditions. Alarms can alert developers to potential issues or anomalies, allowing them to take proactive action to address them.
- **Dashboards**: AWS CloudWatch Dashboards provide customizable dashboards for visualizing and monitoring metrics, logs, and alarms in a single view. Dashboards can be used to create custom visualizations and track key performance indicators (KPIs) for serverless applications.

Example:

```python
# Example of logging and monitoring with AWS CloudWatch in Python using AWS Lambda

import json
```

```python
import boto3
import logging
# Initialize AWS SDK clients
cloudwatch = boto3.client('cloudwatch')
logger = logging.getLogger()
logger.setLevel(logging.INFO)
def lambda_handler(event, context):
    # Log event data
    logger.info(f'Received event: {json.dumps(event)}')
    # Send custom metric to CloudWatch
    cloudwatch.put_metric_data(
        Namespace='MyNamespace',
        MetricData=[
            {
                'MetricName': 'CustomMetric',
                'Value': 1,
                'Unit': 'Count'
```

```
    }
    # Process event
    return {
        'statusCode': 200,
        'body': 'Hello, World!'
    }
```

2. Debugging Tools:

In addition to monitoring, debugging tools are essential for identifying and resolving issues in serverless applications. AWS X-Ray is a debugging and tracing service provided by AWS that allows developers to analyze and debug distributed applications, including serverless applications built with AWS Lambda.

Key Features of AWS X-Ray:

- **Tracing**: AWS X-Ray provides end-to-end tracing for requests as they flow through a serverless application, allowing developers to visualize the entire request lifecycle and identify performance bottlenecks or errors.
- **Segmentation**: AWS X-Ray segments requests into individual components, such as function invocations, API calls, and database queries,

making it easier to pinpoint the source of issues and optimize performance.
- **Analytics**: AWS X-Ray offers analytics and insights into application performance, including response times, error rates, and resource utilization. Developers can use these insights to optimize application performance and improve user experience.
- **Integration**: AWS X-Ray integrates seamlessly with AWS Lambda and other AWS services, allowing developers to enable tracing and debugging with minimal configuration.

Example:

```python
# Example of distributed tracing with AWS X-Ray in Python using AWS Lambda

import json

import boto3

from aws_xray_sdk.core import xray_recorder

from aws_xray_sdk.core import patch

# Patch all supported libraries to enable X-Ray tracing

patch(['boto3'])

# Initialize AWS SDK clients
```

```
s3 = boto3.client('s3')

# Decorate Lambda handler function with X-Ray tracing
@xray_recorder.capture('lambda_handler')
def lambda_handler(event, context):
    # Process event
    response = s3.list_buckets()
    # Log response
    print(response)
    return {
        'statusCode': 200,
        'body': json.dumps('Hello, World!')
    }
```

Monitoring and debugging tools are essential for maintaining and troubleshooting serverless applications. AWS CloudWatch and AWS X-Ray provide powerful features for monitoring metrics, analyzing logs, setting up alarms, and tracing requests in serverless applications built with AWS Lambda. By leveraging these tools and best practices, developers can gain insights into the performance and behavior of their applications, identify and resolve issues quickly, and optimize application performance for better user experience. Whether you're monitoring metrics, analyzing logs, setting up alarms, or tracing requests, AWS CloudWatch and AWS X-Ray offer comprehensive solutions for monitoring and debugging serverless applications in the cloud.

Chapter 5

What is the API Gateway Pattern? Centralized Management and Security

The API Gateway pattern is a design approach commonly used in microservices architectures to provide a centralized entry point for accessing backend services and resources. In this article, we'll explore the API Gateway pattern, its benefits, and how it facilitates centralized management and security in serverless applications. We'll provide code examples based on microservices design patterns to illustrate how the API Gateway pattern can be implemented in practice.

1. Introduction to the API Gateway Pattern:

The API Gateway pattern involves using a single entry point to expose a set of APIs that encapsulate the functionality of multiple backend services. Instead of clients directly calling individual services, they interact with the API Gateway, which then routes requests to the appropriate backend service. This pattern promotes loose coupling, simplifies client-server communication, and provides a layer of abstraction between clients and services.

2. Benefits of the API Gateway Pattern:

- **Centralized Management:** The API Gateway serves as a centralized point for managing APIs, allowing developers to define, deploy, and

version APIs in a unified manner. This simplifies API management tasks such as monitoring, logging, authentication, and authorization.
- **Security**: The API Gateway provides a security layer for protecting backend services from unauthorized access and attacks. It can enforce authentication and authorization policies, validate input data, and sanitize requests before forwarding them to backend services.
- **Scalability**: By offloading tasks such as request routing, load balancing, and caching from backend services to the API Gateway, it can improve the scalability and performance of the overall system. The API Gateway can handle spikes in traffic and distribute requests efficiently to backend services.

3. Implementation of the API Gateway Pattern:

In serverless applications, the API Gateway pattern is often implemented using managed API Gateway services provided by cloud providers, such as Amazon API Gateway or Azure API Management. These services offer features for defining, deploying, and managing APIs, as well as integrating with other cloud services and backend systems.

Example:

```yaml
# Example configuration for defining APIs with Amazon API Gateway in AWS SAM
```

```yaml
Resources:
  MyApi:
    Type: AWS::Serverless::Api
    Properties:
      StageName: Prod
      DefinitionBody:
        swagger: "2.0"
        info:
          title: "My API"
          version: "1.0"
        paths:
          /resource1:
            get:
              responses:
                200:
                  description: "Successful response"
          /resource2:
```

```
    post:
      responses:
        200:
          description: "Successful response"
```

4. Centralized Management with API Gateway:

The API Gateway provides a unified interface for managing APIs, allowing developers to define API specifications, configure routing rules, and set up authentication and authorization policies. It offers features such as API versioning, stage management, and deployment automation to streamline the API management lifecycle.

Example:

```yaml
# Example configuration for managing APIs with Amazon API Gateway in AWS SAM

Resources:
  MyApi:
    Type: AWS::Serverless::Api
    Properties:
```

      StageName: Prod

      DefinitionUri: s3://bucket/api-definition.yaml
```

**5. Security with API Gateway:**

The API Gateway enforces security measures to protect backend services from unauthorized access and attacks. It supports authentication methods such as API keys, IAM roles, OAuth, and custom authorizers to authenticate and authorize clients before allowing access to APIs. It also provides features such as request validation and input transformation to sanitize input data and prevent injection attacks.

**Example**:

```yaml

# Example configuration for securing APIs with Amazon API Gateway in AWS SAM

Resources:

  MyApi:

    Type: AWS::Serverless::Api

    Properties:

      Auth:

```
      ApiKeyRequired: true

    DefinitionBody:

      swagger: "2.0"

      info:

        title: "My API"

        version: "1.0"

      paths:

        /resource:

          get:

            responses:

              200:

                description: "Successful response"
```

The API Gateway pattern provides a centralized and secure way to expose APIs in microservices architectures. By using a single entry point for accessing backend services, it simplifies client-server communication, promotes loose coupling, and enables centralized management and security. In serverless applications, managed API Gateway services offered by cloud providers make it easy to implement the API

Gateway pattern and leverage its benefits for building scalable, efficient, and secure microservices-based architectures.

Benefits of API Gateway: Streamlining Access and Simplifying Development

The API Gateway is a crucial component in microservices architectures, serving as a centralized entry point for accessing backend services and resources. It offers a range of benefits that streamline access and simplify development in serverless applications. In this article, we'll explore the key benefits of using an API Gateway and provide code examples based on microservices design patterns to illustrate how it enhances the development process.

1. Centralized Entry Point:

One of the primary benefits of an API Gateway is that it provides a centralized entry point for accessing backend services and resources. Instead of clients directly calling individual services, they interact with the API Gateway, which then routes requests to the appropriate backend service. This promotes loose coupling between clients and services and simplifies client-server communication.

Example:

```yaml

# Example configuration for defining APIs with Amazon API Gateway in AWS SAM
```

```yaml
Resources:
  MyApi:
    Type: AWS::Serverless::Api
    Properties:
      StageName: Prod
      DefinitionBody:
        swagger: "2.0"
        info:
          title: "My API"
          version: "1.0"
        paths:
          /resource1:
            get:
              responses:
                200:
                  description: "Successful response"
          /resource2:
```

```
      post:
        responses:
          200:
            description: "Successful response"
```

2. Simplified Client-Side Development:

By providing a unified interface for accessing backend services, the API Gateway simplifies client-side development. Clients only need to know the URL and endpoints of the API Gateway, rather than the specific details of each backend service. This reduces complexity and allows clients to interact with the API Gateway using standard HTTP methods and protocols.

Example:

```python
# Example of interacting with an API Gateway in Python using requests library

import requests

url = 'https://api.example.com'

endpoint = '/resource1'

response = requests.get(url + endpoint)
```

```
data = response.json()

print(data)
```
```

**3. Protocol Translation and Transformation:**

The API Gateway can perform protocol translation and data transformation to adapt requests and responses between different formats and protocols. For example, it can transform requests from HTTP to HTTPS, or from XML to JSON, and vice versa. This enables clients and services to communicate using their preferred formats and protocols without requiring changes to the underlying systems.

**Example**:

```yaml
# Example configuration for protocol translation and transformation with Amazon API Gateway in AWS SAM

Resources:
  MyApi:
    Type: AWS::Serverless::Api
    Properties:
      StageName: Prod
```
```

```
DefinitionBody:
  swagger: "2.0"
  info:
    title: "My API"
    version: "1.0"
  paths:
    /resource:
      post:
        produces:
          - application/xml
        responses:
          200:
            description: "Successful response"
```

4. Security and Authentication:

The API Gateway provides built-in security features for protecting backend services from unauthorized access and attacks. It can enforce authentication and authorization policies, validate input data, and sanitize requests before forwarding them to backend services. This ensures that only authenticated and authorized clients can access protected resources.

Example:

```yaml
# Example configuration for securing APIs with Amazon API Gateway in AWS SAM
Resources:
  MyApi:
    Type: AWS::Serverless::Api
    Properties:
      Auth:
        ApiKeyRequired: true
      DefinitionBody:
        swagger: "2.0"
        info:
          title: "My API"
          version: "1.0"
        paths:
```

```
    /resource:
      get:
        responses:
          200:
            description: "Successful response"
```

5. Scalability and Performance:

By offloading tasks such as request routing, load balancing, and caching from backend services to the API Gateway, it can improve the scalability and performance of the overall system. The API Gateway can handle spikes in traffic and distribute requests efficiently to backend services, ensuring optimal performance and responsiveness.

Example:

```yaml
# Example configuration for caching with Amazon API Gateway in AWS SAM
Resources:
  MyApi:
    Type: AWS::Serverless::Api
```

```
  Properties:
    CacheClusterEnabled: true
    CacheClusterSize: "0.5"
    DefinitionBody:
      swagger: "2.0"
      info:
        title: "My API"
        version: "1.0"
      paths:
        /resource:
          get:
            responses:
              200:
                description: "Successful response"
```

The API Gateway offers several benefits for streamlining access and simplifying development in serverless applications. By providing a centralized entry point, simplifying client-side development, performing protocol translation and transformation, enforcing security and authentication, and improving scalability and performance, the API Gateway enhances the development process and enables developers to build scalable, efficient, and secure microservices-based architectures. Whether you're building a small prototype or a large-scale production application, leveraging the API Gateway can help you streamline access to backend services and simplify development in serverless applications.

Implementing the API Gateway Pattern with Serverless Technologies

The API Gateway pattern is a fundamental architectural design approach in microservices architectures, enabling centralized access and management of APIs. Leveraging serverless technologies, such as AWS Lambda and Amazon API Gateway, provides a powerful and scalable platform for implementing the API Gateway pattern. In this article, we'll explore how to implement the API Gateway pattern with serverless technologies, including code examples based on microservices design patterns for serverless applications.

1. Introduction to the API Gateway Pattern:

The API Gateway pattern involves using a single entry point to expose a set of APIs that encapsulate the functionality of multiple backend services. This pattern promotes loose coupling between clients and services, simplifies client-server communication, and provides a layer of abstraction for managing and securing APIs.

2. Implementing API Gateway with AWS Lambda and Amazon API Gateway:

Amazon API Gateway is a fully managed service provided by AWS for creating, publishing, maintaining, monitoring, and securing APIs at any scale. Combined with AWS Lambda, which provides serverless compute power, it offers a powerful platform for implementing the API Gateway pattern in serverless applications.

Example:

```yaml
# Example configuration for defining APIs with Amazon API Gateway and AWS Lambda in AWS SAM

Resources:
  MyApi:
    Type: AWS::Serverless::Api
    Properties:
      StageName: Prod
      DefinitionBody:
        swagger: "2.0"
```

```yaml
info:
  title: "My API"
  version: "1.0"
paths:
  /resource1:
    get:
      x-amazon-apigateway-integration:
        type: "aws_proxy"
        uri: !Sub "arn:aws:apigateway:${AWS::Region}:lambda:path/2015-03-31/functions/${MyFunction1.Arn}/invocations"
      responses:
        200:
          description: "Successful response"
  /resource2:
    post:
      x-amazon-apigateway-integration:
        type: "aws_proxy"
```

```
            uri: !Sub
"arn:aws:apigateway:${AWS::Region}:lambda:path/201
5-03-31/functions/${MyFunction2.Arn}/invocations"

          responses:

            200:

              description: "Successful response"
  MyFunction1:
    Type: AWS::Serverless::Function
    Properties:
      Handler: index.handler
      Runtime: nodejs14.x
      CodeUri: .
      Events:
        MyApi:
          Type: Api
          Properties:
            Path: /resource1
            Method: get
```

```
  MyFunction2:
    Type: AWS::Serverless::Function
    Properties:
      Handler: index.handler
      Runtime: nodejs14.x
      CodeUri: .
      Events:
        MyApi:
          Type: Api
          Properties:
            Path: /resource2
            Method: post
```

3. Benefits of Implementing API Gateway with Serverless Technologies:

- **Scalability**: AWS Lambda and Amazon API Gateway are fully managed services that automatically scale to handle any amount of traffic, ensuring high availability and reliability for APIs.

- **Cost Efficiency:** With serverless technologies, you only pay for the compute resources used when executing functions and handling requests, resulting in cost savings compared to traditional server-based architectures.
- **Simplified Management:** Serverless technologies abstract away infrastructure management tasks, allowing developers to focus on building and deploying APIs without worrying about provisioning, scaling, or maintenance.
- **Integration with AWS Ecosystem:** AWS Lambda and Amazon API Gateway seamlessly integrate with other AWS services, such as Amazon DynamoDB, Amazon S3, and AWS IAM, enabling developers to build powerful and scalable serverless applications with ease.

4. Microservices Design Patterns with API Gateway:

When implementing the API Gateway pattern with serverless technologies, it's essential to follow microservices design patterns to build scalable, efficient, and maintainable applications. Some common microservices design patterns include:

- **Authentication and Authorization:** Implementing authentication and authorization mechanisms at the API Gateway level to enforce security policies and protect backend services from unauthorized access.
- **Service Discovery:** Using service discovery mechanisms to dynamically route requests to

backend services based on service availability, load, or other factors.
- **Circuit Breaker:** Implementing circuit breaker patterns to handle failures gracefully and prevent cascading failures across the system.
- **Event-Driven Architecture:** Leveraging event-driven architecture to decouple services and enable asynchronous communication between components.

Implementing the API Gateway pattern with serverless technologies, such as AWS Lambda and Amazon API Gateway, offers a scalable, cost-effective, and simplified approach to building APIs in microservices architectures. By leveraging the benefits of serverless computing, developers can focus on building and deploying APIs without worrying about infrastructure management, while following microservices design patterns to ensure scalability, reliability, and maintainability of their serverless applications. Whether you're building a small prototype or a large-scale production application, implementing the API Gateway pattern with serverless technologies provides a flexible and powerful platform for building modern, cloud-native applications.

Best Practices for Designing Effective APIs for Microservices

Designing effective APIs for microservices is crucial for building scalable, maintainable, and interoperable systems. In this article, we'll explore best practices for designing APIs in the context of microservices architecture, with a focus on serverless applications. We'll discuss key principles, patterns, and code examples based on microservices design patterns to illustrate how to create robust and efficient APIs for microservices.

1. RESTful API Design:

RESTful APIs are a widely adopted standard for designing web APIs that are scalable, maintainable, and easy to understand. When designing APIs for microservices, it's essential to follow RESTful principles, such as using HTTP methods (GET, POST, PUT, DELETE) to perform CRUD operations, resource-based URIs, and stateless communication.

Example:

```yaml
# Example of a RESTful API definition for a user service in AWS SAM

Resources:
  UserApi:
    Type: AWS::Serverless::Api
    Properties:
      StageName: Prod
      DefinitionBody:
```

```yaml
swagger: "2.0"
info:
  title: "User API"
  version: "1.0"
paths:
  /users:
    get:
      responses:
        200:
          description: "Successful response"
```

2. Versioning:

API versioning is essential for managing changes and backward compatibility in microservices architectures. It's recommended to include version information in the URI or headers of the API requests to ensure that clients can specify the desired version and handle changes gracefully.

Example:

```yaml
```

```yaml
# Example of versioning in API URI for a user service in AWS SAM
Resources:
  UserApi:
    Type: AWS::Serverless::Api
    Properties:
      StageName: Prod
      DefinitionBody:
        swagger: "2.0"
        info:
          title: "User API"
          version: "1.0"
        paths:
          /v1/users:
            get:
              responses:
                200:
                  description: "Successful response"
```

```

### 3. Use of HTTP Status Codes:

Proper use of HTTP status codes is essential for communicating the outcome of API requests to clients. Use standard HTTP status codes (e.g., 200 for success, 404 for not found, 500 for server errors) to provide meaningful responses and help clients understand the outcome of their requests.

**Example**:

```javascript

// Example of returning HTTP status codes in an API response handler

exports.handler = async (event) => {

    // Process request

    // ...

    return {

        statusCode: 200,

        body: JSON.stringify({ message: 'Resource created successfully' }),

    };

```
```

4. Error Handling:

Effective error handling is crucial for providing a good developer experience and debugging issues in microservices. Use consistent error formats and provide descriptive error messages to help clients diagnose and troubleshoot problems.

Example:

```javascript
// Example of error handling in an API response handler
exports.handler = async (event) => {
  try {
    // Process request
    // ...
    return {
      statusCode: 200,
      body: JSON.stringify({ message: 'Resource created successfully' }),
    };
  } catch (error) {
    // Handle error
```

```
    return {
        statusCode: 500,
        body: JSON.stringify({ message: 'Internal server error' }),
    };
```
```

## 5. Authentication and Authorization:

Implement authentication and authorization mechanisms to protect APIs from unauthorized access and ensure data security. Use industry-standard authentication protocols such as OAuth 2.0 or JWT tokens, and enforce access controls based on user roles and permissions.

**Example**:

```yaml
# Example of authentication and authorization configuration for an API in AWS SAM
Resources:
  MyApi:
    Type: AWS::Serverless::Api
    Properties:
```
```

```
  Auth:
    DefaultAuthorizer: MyAuthorizer
    Authorizers:
      MyAuthorizer:
        Type: COGNITO_USER_POOLS
        ProviderARNs:
          - arn:aws:cognito-idp:us-east-1:123456789012:userpool/us-east-1_aBC123
```

6. Documentation:

Provide comprehensive documentation for APIs to help developers understand how to use them effectively. Include information such as endpoints, request parameters, response formats, authentication requirements, and usage examples to make it easy for developers to integrate with your APIs.

Example:

```markdown
# User API

**Get Users**
```

- **Endpoint**: `/users`
- **Method**: `GET`
- **Description**: Retrieve a list of users.
- **Authentication**: Required

```

Designing effective APIs for microservices is essential for building scalable, maintainable, and interoperable systems. By following best practices such as RESTful API design, versioning, proper use of HTTP status codes, error handling, authentication and authorization, and documentation, developers can create robust and efficient APIs that meet the requirements of modern microservices architectures. Whether you're building a small prototype or a large-scale production application, implementing these best practices will help you design APIs that are scalable, secure, and easy to use.
```

Chapter 6

Understanding Event-Driven Architecture: Microservices Reacting to Events

Event-driven architecture (EDA) is a design pattern commonly used in microservices architectures to enable asynchronous communication and decouple components. In this article, we'll explore the principles of event-driven architecture, how microservices react to events, and provide code examples based on microservices design patterns for serverless applications.

1. Introduction to Event-Driven Architecture:

Event-driven architecture is a design paradigm where components of a system communicate by generating and consuming events. Events represent significant occurrences or changes in the system, such as user actions, system alerts, or data updates. Instead of direct communication between components, events are published to a central event bus or message broker, allowing interested components to react to them asynchronously.

2. Key Concepts in Event-Driven Architecture:

- **Events**: Events are messages that represent significant occurrences or changes in the system. They typically consist of a payload containing relevant data and metadata such as event type, timestamp, and source.

- **Event Producer:** An event producer is a component that generates and publishes events to the event bus. It can be any part of the system that produces events, such as a user interface, backend service, or external system.
- **Event Consumer:** An event consumer is a component that subscribes to events from the event bus and reacts to them. It processes incoming events, performs actions or updates state based on the event content.
- **Event Bus:** The event bus is a central communication channel that facilitates the exchange of events between producers and consumers. It acts as a mediator, ensuring that events are delivered to the appropriate consumers based on their subscriptions.

3. Implementing Event-Driven Architecture in Microservices:

In a microservices architecture, each microservice can act as both an event producer and an event consumer. Microservices can generate events to notify other services of changes or trigger actions based on incoming events from other services. This decouples services, promotes scalability and resilience, and enables flexible composition of systems.

Example:

```python
```

```
# Example of publishing an event in a microservice using AWS Lambda and Amazon EventBridge

import json

import boto3

event_bridge = boto3.client('events')

def publish_event(event_type, payload):
    response = event_bridge.put_events(
        Entries=[
            {
                'Source': 'my-service',
                'DetailType': event_type,
                'Detail': json.dumps(payload)
            }
        ]
    return response
```
```

## 4. Microservices Design Patterns for Event-Driven Architecture:

Several design patterns are commonly used in event-driven microservices architectures to handle different
```

types of events and ensure reliable communication between services:

- **Event Sourcing:** Store events as a log of changes to the system's state, allowing services to replay events and rebuild state as needed.
- **CQRS (Command Query Responsibility Segregation):** Separate the read and write operations of a system, enabling services to optimize for different use cases and scalability requirements.
- **Saga Pattern:** Coordinate distributed transactions across multiple services by using a series of compensating actions to ensure eventual consistency.

5. Benefits of Event-Driven Architecture:

Event-driven architecture offers several benefits for building scalable, resilient, and loosely coupled systems:

- **Decoupling**: Components can interact with each other without needing to know about the internal implementation details, leading to loose coupling and improved flexibility.
- **Scalability**: Asynchronous communication allows components to scale independently, enabling better resource utilization and performance optimization.
- **Resilience**: Services can continue to operate independently even if other components are unavailable or experiencing failures, enhancing system resilience and fault tolerance.

6. Challenges of Event-Driven Architecture:

While event-driven architecture offers many benefits, it also presents challenges such as:

- **Event Ordering:** Ensuring the correct ordering of events across distributed systems can be challenging, especially in scenarios with high concurrency or network partitions.
- **Eventual Consistency:** Achieving eventual consistency across distributed systems may require careful coordination and handling of race conditions and conflicts.
- **Debugging and Monitoring:** Debugging and monitoring event-driven systems can be more complex than traditional request-response architectures due to the asynchronous nature of event processing.

Event-driven architecture is a powerful design pattern for building scalable, resilient, and loosely coupled microservices architectures. By leveraging events as the primary means of communication between components, developers can create flexible, decoupled systems that can scale and evolve over time. Whether you're building a small application or a large-scale distributed system, understanding the principles of event-driven architecture and applying microservices design patterns will help you design robust and efficient serverless applications.

Benefits of Event-Driven Architecture: Scalability, Loose Coupling, and Flexibility

Event-Driven Architecture (EDA) is a powerful design pattern that enables asynchronous communication between components in a system. By using events to trigger and handle actions, Event-Driven Architecture offers several benefits, including scalability, loose coupling, and flexibility. In this article, we'll delve into these benefits, provide code examples based on microservices design patterns for serverless applications, and explore how Event-Driven Architecture enhances the development and operation of modern systems.

1. Scalability:

One of the primary benefits of Event-Driven Architecture is its inherent scalability. By decoupling components and enabling asynchronous communication via events, systems built using EDA can scale horizontally to handle increased loads without requiring changes to the architecture. Each component can independently scale based on its specific workload, allowing for optimal resource utilization and improved performance.

Example:

```python
# Example of scaling event-driven microservices with AWS Lambda and Amazon EventBridge
```

```python
import json

import boto3

event_bridge = boto3.client('events')

def publish_event(event_type, payload):
    response = event_bridge.put_events(
        Entries=[
            {
                'Source': 'my-service',
                'DetailType': event_type,
                'Detail': json.dumps(payload)
            }
        ]
    return response
```

2. Loose Coupling:

Event-Driven Architecture promotes loose coupling between components by removing direct dependencies and enabling communication through events. Components can interact with each other without needing to know the internal implementation details of other services. This loose coupling enhances system resilience, as changes or updates to one component are less likely to impact other components, making it easier to maintain and evolve the system over time.

Example:

```python
# Example of handling events in a microservice using AWS Lambda and Amazon EventBridge

def handle_event(event, context):
    # Process event
    payload = event['detail']
    # Perform actions based on the event
```

3. Flexibility:

Event-Driven Architecture provides flexibility in system design and development by allowing components to react to events dynamically. New functionality can be added by introducing new event handlers or subscribers without needing to modify existing components. This flexibility enables developers to iterate quickly, experiment with different features, and adapt to changing requirements without disrupting the entire system.

Example:

```python

# Example of adding a new event handler in a microservice using AWS Lambda and Amazon EventBridge

def new_event_handler(event, context):

    # Process new event

    payload = event['detail']

    # Perform actions based on the new event

```

4. Microservices Design Patterns for Event-Driven Architecture:

Several microservices design patterns complement Event-Driven Architecture and enhance its benefits:

- **Event Sourcing:** Store events as a log of changes to the system's state, enabling services to replay events and rebuild state as needed.
- **CQRS (Command Query Responsibility Segregation):** Separate the read and write operations of a system, enabling services to optimize for different use cases and scalability requirements.
- **Saga Pattern:** Coordinate distributed transactions across multiple services by using a

series of compensating actions to ensure eventual consistency.

Event-Driven Architecture offers numerous benefits, including scalability, loose coupling, and flexibility, making it an ideal choice for building modern, distributed systems. By leveraging events as the primary means of communication between components, developers can create scalable, resilient, and adaptable systems that can evolve and grow over time. Whether you're building a small application or a large-scale distributed system, Event-Driven Architecture and microservices design patterns provide a robust foundation for building serverless applications that meet the demands of today's dynamic business environments.

Implementing Event-Driven Microservices with Serverless and Event Queues (e.g., SQS)

Event-driven microservices architecture, when combined with serverless computing and event queues such as Amazon Simple Queue Service (SQS), offers a scalable and resilient solution for building modern applications. In this article, we'll explore the principles of event-driven microservices, discuss the benefits of using serverless and event queues, and provide code examples based on microservices design patterns for serverless applications.

1. Introduction to Event-Driven Microservices:

Event-driven microservices architecture is based on the concept of components communicating through events.

Each microservice is responsible for handling specific events, triggering actions, and producing new events. This approach promotes loose coupling, scalability, and resilience, as services can operate independently and react to changes asynchronously.

2. Benefits of Event-Driven Microservices with Serverless and Event Queues:

- **Scalability**: Serverless computing platforms like AWS Lambda automatically scale based on demand, allowing event-driven microservices to handle varying workloads efficiently.
- **Resilience**: Event queues such as SQS provide reliable message delivery, ensuring that events are processed even if services are temporarily unavailable or experiencing failures.
- **Loose Coupling:** By decoupling components and communicating through events, event-driven microservices reduce dependencies and make it easier to evolve and maintain the system over time.

3. Implementing Event-Driven Microservices with AWS Lambda and SQS:

Amazon Web Services (AWS) offers a comprehensive suite of services for building event-driven microservices. Let's explore how to implement event-driven microservices using AWS Lambda and SQS:

Example:

```python
# Example of an event-driven microservice using AWS Lambda and SQS

import json
import boto3

sqs = boto3.client('sqs')

def handler(event, context):
    # Process incoming event
    payload = event['detail']

    # Perform actions based on the event

    # Produce new event
    response = sqs.send_message(
        QueueUrl='queue_url',
        MessageBody=json.dumps({'type': 'new_event', 'payload': payload})
    )

    return {
        'statusCode': 200,
```

```
    'body': json.dumps('Event processed successfully')

}
```

4. Microservices Design Patterns for Event-Driven Architecture:

Several microservices design patterns complement event-driven architecture and enhance its benefits:

- **Event Sourcing:** Store events as a log of changes to the system's state, enabling services to replay events and rebuild state as needed.
- **CQRS (Command Query Responsibility Segregation):** Separate the read and write operations of a system, enabling services to optimize for different use cases and scalability requirements.
- **Saga Pattern:** Coordinate distributed transactions across multiple services by using a series of compensating actions to ensure eventual consistency.

5. Using AWS SQS for Event Queues:

Amazon SQS is a fully managed message queuing service that enables decoupling and scaling of microservices. It provides reliable message delivery, scalable message queuing, and built-in redundancy to ensure high availability.

Example:

```python
# Example of receiving messages from an SQS queue in a microservice using AWS Lambda

def handler(event, context):
    for record in event['Records']:
        # Process incoming message
        payload = json.loads(record['body'])
        # Perform actions based on the message
        # ...
    return {
        'statusCode': 200,
        'body': json.dumps('Messages processed successfully')
    }
```

Implementing event-driven microservices with serverless computing and event queues such as AWS SQS offers a scalable, resilient, and loosely coupled solution for building modern applications. By leveraging serverless platforms and event-driven architecture, developers can focus on building business logic without worrying about infrastructure management, while event queues ensure reliable message delivery and decouple components effectively. Whether you're building a small prototype or a large-scale production application, event-driven microservices with serverless and event queues provide a flexible and efficient architecture for meeting the demands of today's dynamic business environments.

Real-World Examples of Event-Driven Microservices (e.g., Order Processing)

Event-driven microservices architecture is widely adopted across various industries to build scalable, resilient, and loosely coupled systems. In this article, we'll explore a real-world example of event-driven microservices for order processing. We'll discuss the architecture, design patterns, and code examples based on microservices design patterns for serverless applications.

1. Introduction to Order Processing:

Order processing is a common scenario in e-commerce and retail industries where customers place orders for products or services. The order processing system typically involves multiple steps, including order creation, payment processing, inventory management, and order fulfillment.

2. Architecture Overview:

The order processing system can be built using an event-driven microservices architecture, where each step in the order processing workflow is implemented as a separate microservice. Events are used to trigger actions and communicate between microservices asynchronously.

3. Microservices Design Patterns for Order Processing:

Several microservices design patterns can be applied to implement the order processing system:

- **Event Sourcing:** Store events as a log of changes to the system's state, enabling services to replay events and rebuild state as needed.
- **CQRS (Command Query Responsibility Segregation):** Separate the read and write operations of a system, enabling services to optimize for different use cases and scalability requirements.
- **Saga Pattern:** Coordinate distributed transactions across multiple services by using a series of compensating actions to ensure eventual consistency.

4. Example Workflow:

Let's break down the order processing workflow into microservices and events:

- **Order Creation Service:** Responsible for creating new orders and publishing an "OrderCreated" event.

- **Payment Service:** Listens for "OrderCreated" events, processes payments, and publishes "PaymentProcessed" events.
- **Inventory Service:** Listens for "OrderCreated" and "PaymentProcessed" events, updates inventory levels, and publishes "InventoryUpdated" events.
- **Shipping Service:** Listens for "InventoryUpdated" events, processes orders for shipping, and publishes "OrderShipped" events.

5. Code Examples:

Let's provide simplified code examples for each microservice:

Order Creation Service:

```python
# Example of order creation service using AWS Lambda and Amazon EventBridge

import json

import boto3

event_bridge = boto3.client('events')

def create_order(order_data):
    # Create order
    # ...
```

```python
# Publish OrderCreated event
event_bridge.put_events(
    Entries=[
        {
            'Source': 'order_service',
            'DetailType': 'OrderCreated',
            'Detail': json.dumps(order_data)
        }
```

Payment Service:

```python
# Example of payment service using AWS Lambda and Amazon EventBridge
def process_payment(event, context):
    # Process payment
    # ...
    # Publish PaymentProcessed event
    # ...
```

```

### **Inventory Service:**

```python

# Example of inventory service using AWS Lambda and Amazon EventBridge

def update_inventory(event, context):

    # Update inventory

    # ...

    # Publish InventoryUpdated event

    # ...
```

Shipping Service:

```python

# Example of shipping service using AWS Lambda and Amazon EventBridge

def process_shipping(event, context):

    # Process shipping

    # ...
```
```

```
    # Publish OrderShipped event

    # ...
```

Event-driven microservices architecture provides a scalable, resilient, and loosely coupled solution for order processing systems. By breaking down the order processing workflow into smaller, independent microservices and using events to trigger actions, developers can build flexible and efficient systems that can adapt to changing requirements and handle varying workloads. Whether you're building an e-commerce platform, a logistics system, or any other order processing application, event-driven microservices offer a powerful architecture for building modern, cloud-native applications.

Chapter 7

The Challenge of Long-Running Tasks: Blocking Microservices and Performance Issues

In microservices architectures, long-running tasks can present significant challenges, leading to blocking microservices and performance issues. These tasks may include operations such as data processing, file uploads, or complex computations that require significant time to complete. In this article, we'll explore the challenges posed by long-running tasks in microservices, discuss their impact on system performance, and propose solutions and design patterns, including examples based on microservices design patterns for serverless applications.

1. Introduction to Long-Running Tasks:

Long-running tasks are operations that take a considerable amount of time to complete, potentially blocking microservices and hindering overall system performance. Examples of long-running tasks include:

- Large data processing or analysis.
- File uploads or downloads.
- Complex computations or algorithms.

2. Challenges of Long-Running Tasks in Microservices:

Long-running tasks can introduce several challenges in microservices architectures:

- **Blocking Microservices:** When a microservice is occupied with a long-running task, it may become unresponsive to other requests, leading to degraded performance and potential downtime for other services that depend on it.
- **Resource Consumption:** Long-running tasks may consume significant resources such as CPU, memory, and network bandwidth, affecting the overall performance and scalability of the system.
- **Timeouts and Failures:** If long-running tasks exceed predefined timeouts, clients may experience timeouts or failures, leading to poor user experience and potential data inconsistency.

3. Impact on System Performance:

The impact of long-running tasks on system performance can be severe, affecting various aspects of the system:

- **Throughput**: Long-running tasks can reduce the overall throughput of the system by occupying resources and delaying the processing of other requests.
- **Latency**: Increased latency due to blocking microservices can lead to slower response times for client requests, affecting user experience and system responsiveness.
- **Scalability**: Long-running tasks may limit the scalability of the system by consuming resources

that could otherwise be used to handle additional workload or scale out horizontally.

4. Solutions and Design Patterns:

Several solutions and design patterns can help mitigate the challenges of long-running tasks in microservices architectures:

- **Asynchronous Processing:** Offload long-running tasks to asynchronous processing queues or background workers to free up microservices and avoid blocking.
- **Event-Driven Architecture:** Use event-driven architecture to decouple components and trigger actions based on events, enabling services to react asynchronously to long-running tasks.
- **Batch Processing:** Break down long-running tasks into smaller, manageable batches to distribute the workload and improve resource utilization.
- **Timeouts and Retries:** Implement timeouts and retries for long-running tasks to prevent indefinite blocking and handle transient failures gracefully.

5. Code Examples:

Let's provide simplified code examples for implementing asynchronous processing with AWS Lambda and Amazon SQS:

```python
```

```python
# Example of asynchronous processing with AWS Lambda and Amazon SQS

import json

import boto3

sqs = boto3.client('sqs')

def process_long_running_task(task_data):
    # Process long-running task
    # ...

def handler(event, context):
    for record in event['Records']:
        task_data = json.loads(record['body'])
        process_long_running_task(task_data)
```

Long-running tasks pose significant challenges in microservices architectures, including blocking microservices and performance issues. By adopting solutions such as asynchronous processing, event-driven architecture, batch processing, and timeouts and retries, developers can mitigate these challenges and build scalable, resilient microservices systems. Whether you're dealing with data processing, file uploads, or complex computations, understanding the impact of long-running tasks and applying appropriate design patterns is essential for building high-performance microservices architectures in serverless applications.

The Async Processing Pattern Explained: Offloading Work for Efficient Microservices

The Async Processing pattern is a powerful design pattern used in microservices architectures to offload long-running or resource-intensive tasks to asynchronous processing mechanisms. By decoupling the execution of tasks from the microservices handling client requests, the Async Processing pattern enhances the scalability, responsiveness, and reliability of microservices-based systems. In this article, we'll delve into the principles of the Async Processing pattern, discuss its benefits, explore implementation strategies, and provide code examples based on microservices design patterns for serverless applications.

1. Introduction to Async Processing:

In microservices architectures, certain tasks, such as data processing, file uploads, or complex computations, may take a considerable amount of time to complete. Performing these tasks synchronously within microservices can lead to blocking behavior, causing degraded performance and hindering the responsiveness of the system. The Async Processing pattern addresses this challenge by offloading long-running tasks to asynchronous processing mechanisms, such as queues or background workers.

2. Benefits of Async Processing:

The Async Processing pattern offers several benefits for microservices architectures:

- **Improved Scalability:** By offloading long-running tasks to separate processing mechanisms, microservices can remain responsive to client requests and scale more efficiently to handle varying workloads.
- **Enhanced Responsiveness:** Offloading tasks asynchronously prevents microservices from becoming blocked, ensuring that they can continue to process incoming requests and maintain low response times for clients.
- **Reliability and Fault Tolerance:** Asynchronous processing mechanisms, such as queues, provide built-in reliability features such as message persistence, retries, and dead-letter queues, improving fault tolerance and error handling in the system.

3. Implementation Strategies:

There are several strategies for implementing the Async Processing pattern in microservices architectures:

1. **Message Queues:** Use message queues, such as Amazon Simple Queue Service (SQS) or Apache Kafka, to decouple the production and consumption of tasks. Microservices produce tasks as messages onto a queue, while worker

processes consume and process them asynchronously.
2. **Background Workers:** Employ background workers or worker pools within microservices to handle asynchronous tasks. Microservices enqueue tasks for processing by background workers, allowing them to continue serving client requests without blocking.
3. **Serverless Functions:** Leverage serverless computing platforms, such as AWS Lambda or Google Cloud Functions, to execute tasks asynchronously. Microservices trigger serverless functions to process tasks in response to events or messages.

4. Code Examples:

Let's provide code examples for implementing the Async Processing pattern using Amazon SQS and AWS Lambda:

Producer Microservice (Enqueuing Tasks):

```python
# Example of a producer microservice enqueuing tasks to Amazon SQS

import boto3

import json

sqs = boto3.client('sqs')
```

```python
def enqueue_task(task_data):
    response = sqs.send_message(
        QueueUrl='queue_url',
        MessageBody=json.dumps(task_data)
    )
    print(f"Task enqueued: {response['MessageId']}")
# Usage
task_data = {'type': 'process_data', 'payload': {...}}
enqueue_task(task_data)
```

Worker Microservice (Dequeuing and Processing Tasks):

```python
# Example of a worker microservice dequeuing and processing tasks from Amazon SQS
import boto3
import json
sqs = boto3.client('sqs')
```

```python
def process_task(task):
    # Process task asynchronously
    print(f"Processing task: {task}")

def poll_and_process_tasks():
    while True:
        response = sqs.receive_message(
            QueueUrl='queue_url',
            MaxNumberOfMessages=1,
            WaitTimeSeconds=20
        )
        if 'Messages' in response:
            for message in response['Messages']:
                task = json.loads(message['Body'])
                process_task(task)
                sqs.delete_message(QueueUrl='queue_url', ReceiptHandle=message['ReceiptHandle'])

# Usage
poll_and_process_tasks()
```

```

The Async Processing pattern is a fundamental design pattern for building efficient and scalable microservices architectures. By offloading long-running tasks to asynchronous processing mechanisms, such as message queues, background workers, or serverless functions, microservices can maintain responsiveness, scalability, and reliability, even under heavy workloads. Whether you're building e-commerce platforms, analytics systems, or real-time applications, incorporating the Async Processing pattern into your microservices architecture can significantly enhance performance and efficiency.

## Implementing Async Processing with Serverless and Work Queues (e.g., SQS, Lambda)

Async Processing is a crucial pattern in microservices architecture for handling long-running tasks efficiently. By leveraging serverless computing and work queues such as Amazon Simple Queue Service (SQS), developers can build scalable and responsive systems that offload tasks asynchronously. In this article, we'll explore how to implement Async Processing with serverless and work queues, discuss its benefits, and provide code examples based on microservices design patterns for serverless applications.

### 1. Introduction to Async Processing:
```

Async Processing is a design pattern where long-running or resource-intensive tasks are offloaded to asynchronous processing mechanisms. This allows microservices to remain responsive to client requests and handle tasks concurrently without blocking. Work queues, such as SQS, serve as intermediaries for distributing tasks among processing units.

2. Benefits of Async Processing with Serverless and Work Queues:

Implementing Async Processing with serverless and work queues offers several benefits:

- **Scalability**: Serverless platforms, like AWS Lambda, automatically scale resources based on demand, enabling efficient handling of varying workloads.
- **Concurrency**: Work queues allow multiple instances of processing units, such as Lambda functions, to work concurrently on tasks, improving throughput and reducing processing time.
- **Fault Tolerance:** Work queues provide built-in reliability features, such as message persistence, retries, and dead-letter queues, ensuring reliable task processing and error handling.

3. Implementation Strategies:

To implement Async Processing with serverless and work queues, follow these steps:

- **Producer Microservice:** Enqueue tasks onto the work queue when long-running tasks are initiated.
- **Worker Microservice:** Poll the work queue for tasks and process them asynchronously using serverless functions or background workers.

4. Code Examples:

Let's provide code examples for implementing Async Processing with AWS Lambda and Amazon SQS:

Producer Microservice (Enqueuing Tasks):

```python
# Example of a producer microservice enqueuing tasks to Amazon SQS

import boto3
import json

sqs = boto3.client('sqs')

def enqueue_task(task_data):
    response = sqs.send_message(
        QueueUrl='queue_url',
        MessageBody=json.dumps(task_data)
    )
```

```python
    print(f"Task enqueued: {response['MessageId']}")

# Usage
task_data = {'type': 'process_data', 'payload': {...}}
enqueue_task(task_data)
```

Worker Microservice (Dequeuing and Processing Tasks with AWS Lambda):

```python
# Example of a worker microservice dequeuing and processing tasks from Amazon SQS using AWS Lambda
import boto3
import json

sqs = boto3.client('sqs')

def process_task(event, context):
    for record in event['Records']:
        task_data = json.loads(record['body'])
        # Process task asynchronously
        print(f"Processing task: {task_data}")
```

```
# Usage

# AWS Lambda function triggers automatically when
messages are available in the SQS queue
```
```

**5. Integration with AWS Lambda:**

To integrate AWS Lambda with Amazon SQS, create an SQS trigger for the Lambda function. When messages are available in the SQS queue, Lambda will automatically invoke the function to process the tasks.

Implementing Async Processing with serverless and work queues, such as AWS Lambda and Amazon SQS, enables developers to build scalable and responsive microservices architectures. By offloading long-running tasks to asynchronous processing mechanisms, microservices can maintain high performance, reliability, and fault tolerance, even under heavy workloads. Whether you're building e-commerce platforms, data processing pipelines, or real-time applications, leveraging Async Processing with serverless and work queues is a fundamental approach for building efficient and scalable serverless applications.

## Best Practices for Designing Microservices for Asynchronous Work

Designing microservices for asynchronous work is essential for building scalable, resilient, and responsive systems. By leveraging asynchronous processing
```

mechanisms, such as message queues and background workers, developers can offload long-running or resource-intensive tasks and maintain high performance and reliability in microservices architectures. In this article, we'll discuss best practices for designing microservices for asynchronous work, including patterns, principles, and code examples based on microservices design patterns for serverless applications.

1. Understand Asynchronous Workloads:

Before designing microservices for asynchronous work, it's essential to understand the nature of asynchronous workloads and identify tasks that can benefit from asynchronous processing. Long-running tasks, batch processing, event-driven workflows, and resource-intensive computations are typical examples of workloads suitable for asynchronous processing.

2. Decouple Components with Message Queues:

Use message queues, such as Amazon Simple Queue Service (SQS) or Apache Kafka, to decouple components in microservices architectures. Instead of directly invoking downstream services synchronously, microservices produce messages onto a queue, allowing downstream services to consume messages and process them asynchronously.

Example:

```python
```

```python
# Example of enqueuing tasks onto a message queue
import boto3
import json
sqs = boto3.client('sqs')
def enqueue_task(task_data):
    response = sqs.send_message(
        QueueUrl='queue_url',
        MessageBody=json.dumps(task_data)
    )
    print(f"Task enqueued: {response['MessageId']}")
# Usage
task_data = {'type': 'process_data', 'payload': {...}}
enqueue_task(task_data)
```

3. Design Fault-Tolerant Systems:

Design microservices for fault tolerance by incorporating retry mechanisms, error handling, and dead-letter queues. Retries can help mitigate transient failures, while dead-letter queues capture messages that couldn't be processed after a specified number of retries, allowing for manual inspection and resolution.

4. Scale Out Horizontally:

Design microservices to scale out horizontally by distributing workload across multiple instances or containers. Asynchronous processing enables microservices to handle varying workloads efficiently, allowing for seamless scaling as demand increases.

5. Monitor and Measure Performance:

Implement monitoring and performance metrics to track the health and performance of asynchronous workloads. Use tools like Amazon CloudWatch or Prometheus to monitor queue metrics, message processing times, and error rates, enabling proactive detection and resolution of issues.

6. Implement Back Pressure Mechanisms:

Implement backpressure mechanisms to prevent overwhelming downstream services with a high volume of messages. Use techniques such as throttling, rate limiting, or circuit breakers to control the flow of messages and ensure the stability and reliability of the system.

7. Leverage Serverless Computing:

Leverage serverless computing platforms, such as AWS Lambda or Google Cloud Functions, to implement asynchronous workloads without managing infrastructure. Serverless functions automatically scale based on demand and provide built-in integrations with message queues for seamless asynchronous processing.

Example:

```python
# Example of processing messages from a message queue using AWS Lambda

import json

def process_message(event, context):
    for record in event['Records']:
        message_body = json.loads(record['body'])
        # Process message asynchronously
        print(f"Processing message: {message_body}")
```

8. Use Idempotent Operations:

Design microservices to perform idempotent operations when processing messages from queues. Idempotent operations ensure that processing the same message multiple times has the same result, reducing the risk of unintended side effects and ensuring data consistency.

9. Ensure Data Integrity and Consistency:

Implement strategies to ensure data integrity and consistency when processing asynchronous workloads. Use transactional messaging patterns, such as the Saga pattern or two-phase commit, to coordinate distributed transactions across multiple microservices and maintain data consistency.

10. Test and Iterate:

Test asynchronous workflows thoroughly, including edge cases, failure scenarios, and scalability tests. Use automated testing frameworks and tools to simulate real-world conditions and validate the reliability and performance of asynchronous processing mechanisms.

Designing microservices for asynchronous work requires careful consideration of architecture, patterns, and best practices. By leveraging message queues, fault tolerance mechanisms, horizontal scaling, and serverless computing, developers can build robust and scalable systems that efficiently handle asynchronous workloads. Incorporating these best practices ensures high performance, reliability, and responsiveness in microservices architectures, enabling organizations to build modern and resilient applications in serverless environments.

Chapter 8

Understanding Fault Tolerance: Protecting Your Application from Failures

Fault tolerance is a critical aspect of designing and building resilient applications that can withstand failures and disruptions. In microservices architectures, where systems are composed of multiple independent components, ensuring fault tolerance is essential for maintaining system reliability and availability. In this article, we'll explore the concept of fault tolerance, discuss its importance in microservices architectures, and provide code examples based on microservices design patterns for serverless applications.

1. Introduction to Fault Tolerance:

Fault tolerance refers to a system's ability to continue operating and providing services even in the presence of failures or errors. It involves designing systems to anticipate and recover from failures gracefully, minimizing downtime and ensuring uninterrupted service delivery.

2. Importance of Fault Tolerance in Microservices Architectures:

In microservices architectures, where systems are composed of numerous interconnected services, failures are inevitable. Ensuring fault tolerance is crucial for maintaining the reliability and availability of the entire system. Fault tolerance enables microservices architectures to:

- **Handle Failures Gracefully:** Microservices should be resilient to failures in other services or external dependencies, ensuring that failures are contained and do not propagate throughout the system.
- **Maintain High Availability:** Fault-tolerant systems can continue operating and providing services even when individual components or services fail, ensuring uninterrupted service delivery to users.

3. Strategies for Achieving Fault Tolerance:

Several strategies can help achieve fault tolerance in microservices architectures:

- **Retry Mechanisms:** Implement retry mechanisms to automatically retry failed operations, such as network requests or database transactions, with backoff and jitter strategies to prevent overwhelming downstream services.
- **Circuit Breaker Pattern:** Use the Circuit Breaker pattern to monitor the status of downstream services and temporarily stop sending requests if they are experiencing failures, preventing cascading failures and allowing services to recover.
- **Timeouts and Timeouts:** Implement timeouts for requests and operations to prevent resources from being tied up indefinitely, enabling services

to fail fast and recover quickly from unresponsive or slow dependencies.

4. Code Examples:

Let's provide code examples for implementing retry mechanisms and the Circuit Breaker pattern in microservices architectures:

Retry Mechanisms:

```python
import requests

from requests.adapters import HTTPAdapter

from requests.packages.urllib3.util.retry import Retry

def retry_request(url):
    session = requests.Session()

    retries = Retry(total=3, backoff_factor=1, status_forcelist=[500, 502, 503, 504])

    session.mount('http://', HTTPAdapter(max_retries=retries))

    response = session.get(url)

    return response
```

Circuit Breaker Pattern:

```python
class CircuitBreaker:
    def __init__(self, max_failures=3, reset_timeout=10):
        self.max_failures = max_failures
        self.reset_timeout = reset_timeout
        self.failures = 0
        self.open = False
        self.last_failure_time = None

    def execute(self, operation):
        if self.open:
            if self.should_reset():
                self.reset()
                return operation()
            else:
                raise CircuitBreakerOpenError("Circuit breaker is open")
        else:
```

```python
        try:
            result = operation()
            self.failures = 0
            return result
        except Exception as e:
            self.failures += 1
            self.last_failure_time = time.time()
            if self.failures >= self.max_failures:
                self.open = True
            raise e

    def should_reset(self):
        return time.time() - self.last_failure_time > self.reset_timeout

    def reset(self):
        self.failures = 0
        self.open = False
        self.last_failure_time = None

# Usage
```

```
def my_operation():
    # Your operation here
    pass

circuit_breaker = CircuitBreaker()

try:
    result = circuit_breaker.execute(my_operation)
except CircuitBreakerOpenError as e:
    # Handle circuit breaker open
    pass
```

5. Monitoring and Alerting:

Implement monitoring and alerting mechanisms to detect failures and performance issues in real-time. Use tools like Amazon CloudWatch or Prometheus to monitor system metrics, set up alarms, and receive notifications when anomalies or failures occur.

6. Continuous Testing and Chaos Engineering:

Practice continuous testing and chaos engineering to proactively identify and address weaknesses and vulnerabilities in the system. Use techniques such as fault injection, chaos monkeys, and automated testing to simulate failures and validate the system's resilience under different scenarios.

Fault tolerance is crucial for ensuring the reliability and availability of microservices architectures. By implementing strategies such as retry mechanisms, the Circuit Breaker pattern, monitoring and alerting, continuous testing, and chaos engineering, developers can build resilient and fault-tolerant systems that can withstand failures and disruptions, providing uninterrupted service delivery to users. Incorporating fault tolerance into microservices architectures is essential for meeting the demands of modern, distributed applications in serverless environments.

The Circuit Breaker Pattern Explained: Detecting and Handling Errors Gracefully

The Circuit Breaker pattern is a powerful design pattern used in microservices architectures to detect and handle errors gracefully. Inspired by electrical engineering concepts, the Circuit Breaker pattern helps prevent cascading failures and enables systems to recover quickly from faults. In this article, we'll explore the Circuit Breaker pattern in detail, discuss its benefits, provide code examples, and explain how it can be applied in microservices design patterns for serverless applications.

1. Understanding the Circuit Breaker Pattern:

The Circuit Breaker pattern is based on the principle of a circuit breaker in electrical systems. In software engineering, the Circuit Breaker acts as a barrier between a caller and a potentially faulty service or resource. It monitors the health of the service and opens the circuit (stops calling the service) if the service becomes unresponsive or experiences failures.

2. Importance of the Circuit Breaker Pattern in Microservices:

In microservices architectures, where systems are composed of numerous interconnected services, failures in one service can cascade to other services, leading to system-wide outages. The Circuit Breaker pattern helps prevent this by isolating failures and providing a mechanism for handling them gracefully, thereby improving the overall resilience and reliability of the system.

3. How the Circuit Breaker Pattern Works:

The Circuit Breaker pattern typically consists of three states: closed, open, and half-open.

- **Closed State:** In the closed state, the Circuit Breaker allows calls to the service as usual. It monitors the service for errors or failures.
- **Open State:** If the number of errors or failures exceeds a predefined threshold, the Circuit Breaker transitions to the open state. In this state, the Circuit Breaker prevents calls to the service and immediately returns an error response to the caller.

- **Half-Open State:** After a certain period of time, the Circuit Breaker transitions to the half-open state. In this state, it allows a limited number of calls to the service to determine if the service has recovered. If these calls are successful, the Circuit Breaker transitions back to the closed state. Otherwise, it remains in the open state.

4. Benefits of the Circuit Breaker Pattern:

The Circuit Breaker pattern offers several benefits in microservices architectures:

- **Fault Isolation:** The Circuit Breaker isolates failures in one service from affecting other services, preventing cascading failures and minimizing the blast radius of failures.
- **Improved Resilience:** By detecting and handling errors gracefully, the Circuit Breaker improves the resilience of the system, enabling it to recover quickly from faults and continue providing services to users.
- **Reduced Response Times:** The Circuit Breaker helps reduce response times for clients by quickly detecting and failing fast in the event of a service failure, preventing clients from waiting indefinitely for unresponsive services.

5. Implementation of the Circuit Breaker Pattern:

Let's provide a code example for implementing the Circuit Breaker pattern in Python:

```python
import time

class CircuitBreaker:
    def __init__(self, failure_threshold=3, reset_timeout=10):
        self.failure_threshold = failure_threshold
        self.reset_timeout = reset_timeout
        self.failures = 0
        self.last_failure_time = None
        self.state = 'closed'

    def execute(self, operation):
        if self.state == 'open':
            if self.should_reset():
                self.reset()
                self.state = 'half-open'
            else:
                raise CircuitBreakerOpenError("Circuit breaker is open")
```

```python
        try:
            result = operation()
            self.failures = 0
            return result
        except Exception as e:
            self.failures += 1
            self.last_failure_time = time.time()
            if self.failures >= self.failure_threshold:
                self.state = 'open'
            raise e

    def should_reset(self):
        return time.time() - self.last_failure_time > self.reset_timeout

    def reset(self):
        self.failures = 0
        self.last_failure_time = None

# Usage
def my_operation():
```

```
    # Your operation here
    pass

circuit_breaker = CircuitBreaker()
try:
    result = circuit_breaker.execute(my_operation)
except CircuitBreakerOpenError as e:
    # Handle circuit breaker open
    pass
```

The Circuit Breaker pattern is a fundamental design pattern for building resilient and fault-tolerant microservices architectures. By isolating failures, handling errors gracefully, and providing mechanisms for recovery, the Circuit Breaker pattern improves the reliability and availability of systems, ensuring uninterrupted service delivery to users. Incorporating the Circuit Breaker pattern into microservices design patterns for serverless applications is essential for meeting the demands of modern, distributed applications and providing a seamless user experience.

Implementing the Circuit Breaker Pattern with Serverless and Monitoring Tools

Implementing the Circuit Breaker pattern in serverless applications is crucial for building resilient and fault-tolerant systems. By combining the Circuit Breaker pattern with serverless computing and monitoring tools, developers can detect and handle errors gracefully, ensuring high availability and reliability of microservices architectures. In this article, we'll explore how to implement the Circuit Breaker pattern with serverless technologies and monitoring tools, provide code examples, and discuss best practices based on microservices design patterns for serverless applications.

1. Introduction to the Circuit Breaker Pattern:

The Circuit Breaker pattern is a design pattern used to handle errors and failures in distributed systems. It acts as a barrier between components and services, monitoring their health and preventing cascading failures by opening the circuit when failures occur. The Circuit Breaker pattern consists of three states: closed, open, and half-open, providing a mechanism for detecting and recovering from failures gracefully.

2. Implementing the Circuit Breaker Pattern with Serverless:

To implement the Circuit Breaker pattern with serverless technologies, such as AWS Lambda or Google Cloud Functions, follow these steps:

- **Integration with Serverless Functions:** Integrate the Circuit Breaker logic into serverless functions to monitor service health and control the flow of requests based on the state of the Circuit Breaker.
- **Utilize Serverless Triggers:** Use serverless triggers, such as API Gateway events or message queue triggers, to invoke serverless functions and execute the Circuit Breaker logic.
- **Implement Retry and Backoff Strategies:** Implement retry and backoff strategies within serverless functions to handle transient errors and retries gracefully before opening the Circuit Breaker.

3. Monitoring and Alerting:

Integrate monitoring and alerting tools, such as Amazon CloudWatch or Google Cloud Monitoring, to track the state of the Circuit Breaker and receive notifications when it transitions between states. Monitor service health metrics, error rates, and latency to detect patterns of failures and trigger Circuit Breaker actions accordingly.

4. Code Examples:

Let's provide a code example for implementing the Circuit Breaker pattern with AWS Lambda and Amazon CloudWatch:

```python
```

```python
import time

import boto3

class CircuitBreaker:

    def __init__(self, failure_threshold=3, reset_timeout=60):

        self.failure_threshold = failure_threshold

        self.reset_timeout = reset_timeout

        self.failures = 0

        self.last_failure_time = None

        self.state = 'closed'

    def execute(self, operation):

        if self.state == 'open':

            if self.should_reset():

                self.reset()

                self.state = 'half-open'

            else:

                raise CircuitBreakerOpenError("Circuit breaker is open")
```

```python
        try:
            result = operation()
            self.failures = 0
            return result
        except Exception as e:
            self.failures += 1
            self.last_failure_time = time.time()
            if self.failures >= self.failure_threshold:
                self.state = 'open'
            raise e

    def should_reset(self):
        return time.time() - self.last_failure_time > self.reset_timeout

    def reset(self):
        self.failures = 0
        self.last_failure_time = None

# AWS Lambda function handler
def lambda_handler(event, context):
```

```
circuit_breaker = CircuitBreaker()

try:
    result = circuit_breaker.execute(my_operation)
    return result
except CircuitBreakerOpenError as e:
    # Handle circuit breaker open
    pass

def my_operation():
    # Your operation here
    pass
```

5. **Best Practices:**

- **Set Appropriate Thresholds:** Adjust the failure threshold and reset timeout parameters based on the characteristics of your application and service dependencies to balance responsiveness and stability.
- **Monitor and Analyze Metrics:** Continuously monitor service health metrics, error rates, and latency to identify patterns of failures and optimize Circuit Breaker parameters accordingly.

- **Implement Exponential Backoff:** Implement exponential backoff and jitter strategies within retry mechanisms to prevent overwhelming downstream services with retry attempts and mitigate congestion during peak traffic periods.

Implementing the Circuit Breaker pattern with serverless technologies and monitoring tools is essential for building resilient and fault-tolerant microservices architectures. By integrating Circuit Breaker logic into serverless functions, utilizing serverless triggers, monitoring service health metrics, and implementing best practices, developers can detect and handle errors gracefully, ensuring high availability and reliability of serverless applications. Incorporating the Circuit Breaker pattern into microservices design patterns for serverless applications is critical for meeting the demands of modern, distributed applications and providing a seamless user experience.

Ensuring Fault Tolerance and High Availability in Your Microservices Architecture

Fault tolerance and high availability are critical aspects of designing and maintaining microservices architectures. In today's distributed computing landscape, where systems are composed of numerous interconnected services, ensuring that individual services can withstand failures and continue operating reliably is paramount. In this article, we'll explore strategies for ensuring fault tolerance and high availability in your microservices architecture, provide code examples, and discuss best practices based on microservices design patterns for serverless applications.

1. Introduction to Fault Tolerance and High Availability:

Fault tolerance refers to a system's ability to continue operating and providing services even in the presence of failures or errors. High availability, on the other hand, refers to the ability of a system to remain operational and accessible for users, typically measured as a percentage of uptime. Both fault tolerance and high availability are essential for building resilient and reliable microservices architectures.

2. Strategies for Ensuring Fault Tolerance and High Availability:

- **Redundancy and Replication:** Deploy multiple instances of critical services across different availability zones or regions to ensure redundancy and fault tolerance. Use load balancers to distribute incoming traffic evenly across instances, enabling high availability and fault tolerance.
- **Health Monitoring and Self-Healing:** Implement health monitoring mechanisms to continuously monitor the health and performance of services. Use automated remediation techniques, such as auto-scaling and self-healing, to automatically replace or restart unhealthy instances and maintain system reliability.

- **Graceful Degradation:** Design services to gracefully degrade functionality under high load or failure conditions. Implement fallback mechanisms, such as caching, circuit breakers, or degraded service modes, to maintain basic functionality and prevent cascading failures.

3. Implementing Fault Tolerance and High Availability with Serverless:

Serverless computing platforms, such as AWS Lambda or Google Cloud Functions, provide built-in features for ensuring fault tolerance and high availability. Leveraging serverless technologies can simplify the implementation of fault tolerance and high availability in your microservices architecture.

- **Automatic Scaling:** Serverless functions automatically scale up or down based on demand, ensuring that your services can handle varying workloads without manual intervention. This enables fault tolerance and high availability by dynamically adjusting resources to meet demand.
- **Managed Services:** Utilize managed services, such as Amazon DynamoDB or Google Cloud Firestore, for storing data with built-in redundancy and replication. Managed services abstract away the complexity of infrastructure management, allowing you to focus on building resilient applications.

4. Code Examples:

Let's provide code examples for implementing fault tolerance and high availability using AWS Lambda and Amazon DynamoDB:

```python
# AWS Lambda function handler
import boto3

dynamodb = boto3.client('dynamodb')

def lambda_handler(event, context):
    try:
        response = dynamodb.put_item(
            TableName='my_table',
            Item={
                'id': {'S': '1'},
                'data': {'S': 'example'}
            }
        )
        return response
    except Exception as e:
        # Handle error gracefully
```

pass

```
```

5. Best Practices:

- **Design for Failure:** Assume that failures will occur and design your microservices architecture with failure in mind. Implement retry mechanisms, circuit breakers, and fallback strategies to handle failures gracefully and prevent cascading failures.
- **Test and Monitor:** Continuously test and monitor your microservices architecture to identify potential points of failure and performance bottlenecks. Implement logging, monitoring, and alerting mechanisms to detect and respond to failures in real-time.
- **Regularly Review and Update:** Regularly review and update your fault tolerance and high availability strategies to adapt to changing requirements and evolving best practices. Incorporate lessons learned from incidents and failures to improve resilience and reliability over time.

Ensuring fault tolerance and high availability in your microservices architecture is essential for building resilient and reliable systems. By implementing redundancy and replication, health monitoring and self-healing, graceful degradation, and leveraging serverless technologies, you can design microservices architectures that can withstand failures and continue providing services to users. Incorporating fault tolerance and high availability strategies based on microservices design patterns for serverless applications is crucial for meeting the demands of modern, distributed applications and delivering a seamless user experience.

Chapter 9

Securing Your Microservices: Authentication, Authorization, and Encryption

Securing microservices is paramount in modern distributed architectures to protect sensitive data, prevent unauthorized access, and ensure the integrity and confidentiality of services. Authentication, authorization, and encryption are fundamental components of a robust security strategy for microservices. In this article, we'll delve into best practices for securing your microservices, provide code examples, and discuss how to implement authentication, authorization, and encryption in microservices design patterns for serverless applications.

1. Introduction to Microservices Security:

Microservices architectures introduce unique security challenges due to their distributed nature, where services communicate over networks and interact with various components and dependencies. Securing microservices involves implementing measures to authenticate users and services, authorize access to resources, and encrypt data to protect it from unauthorized access or tampering.

2. Authentication:

Authentication verifies the identity of users or services accessing microservices. Implementing strong authentication mechanisms ensures that only authorized entities can access resources and perform actions within the system.

Code Example - Authentication with JWT (JSON Web Tokens):

```python
import jwt
from flask import Flask, request
from functools import wraps

app = Flask(__name__)
app.config['SECRET_KEY'] = 'your_secret_key'

def token_required(f):
    @wraps(f)
    def decorated(*args, **kwargs):
        token = request.args.get('token')
        if not token:
            return {'message': 'Token is missing'}, 401
        try:
            data = jwt.decode(token, app.config['SECRET_KEY'])
```

```
        except:
            return {'message': 'Token is invalid'}, 401
        return f(*args, **kwargs)
    return decorated

@app.route('/protected')
@token_required
def protected():
    return {'message': 'Protected resource accessed'}

if __name__ == '__main__':
    app.run()
```

3. Authorization:

Authorization determines what actions users or services are allowed to perform once authenticated. Implementing fine-grained authorization policies ensures that access to resources is restricted based on roles, permissions, or attributes.

Code Example - Role-Based Access Control (RBAC):

```python
```

```python
from flask import Flask, request

app = Flask(__name__)

def is_admin():
    # Logic to determine if user is an admin
    return True

@app.route('/admin')
def admin():
    if not is_admin():
        return {'message': 'Unauthorized'}, 403
    return {'message': 'Admin resource accessed'}

if __name__ == '__main__':
    app.run()
```
```

### 4. Encryption:

Encryption protects sensitive data by encoding it in a way that only authorized entities can decrypt and access. Implementing encryption ensures the confidentiality and integrity of data transmitted and stored within microservices.
```

Code Example - Encrypting Data with AES (Advanced Encryption Standard):

```python
from Crypto.Cipher import AES
from Crypto.Random import get_random_bytes
import base64

def encrypt_data(data, key):
    cipher = AES.new(key, AES.MODE_CBC)
    ct_bytes = cipher.encrypt(data.encode())
    iv = base64.b64encode(cipher.iv).decode('utf-8')
    ct = base64.b64encode(ct_bytes).decode('utf-8')
    return iv, ct

def decrypt_data(iv, ct, key):
    iv = base64.b64decode(iv)
    ct = base64.b64decode(ct)
    cipher = AES.new(key, AES.MODE_CBC, iv)
    pt = cipher.decrypt(ct).decode('utf-8')
    return pt
```

```
# Example usage

key = get_random_bytes(16)

iv, ct = encrypt_data('Hello, world!', key)

pt = decrypt_data(iv, ct, key)

print(pt)

```

5. **Best Practices for Microservices Security:**

- **Implement HTTPS:** Secure communication between microservices and clients using HTTPS to encrypt data in transit and prevent eavesdropping or tampering.
- **Least Privilege Principle:** Follow the principle of least privilege by granting users and services only the permissions necessary to perform their tasks, reducing the attack surface and limiting the impact of potential security breaches.
- **Regular Audits and Penetration Testing:** Conduct regular security audits and penetration testing to identify vulnerabilities and weaknesses in your microservices architecture and address them proactively.
- **Use Secure Libraries and Frameworks:** Use secure libraries and frameworks for implementing authentication, authorization, and encryption to leverage built-in security features and reduce the risk of vulnerabilities.

Securing microservices is essential for protecting sensitive data, ensuring the integrity of services, and maintaining the trust of users and clients. By implementing robust authentication, authorization, and encryption mechanisms, developers can build secure microservices architectures that withstand security threats and mitigate risks effectively. Incorporating best practices and following security principles based on microservices design patterns for serverless applications is crucial for achieving a high level of security and resilience in modern distributed systems.

IAM Policies and Roles for Serverless Functions: Granting Least Privilege

IAM (Identity and Access Management) policies and roles are fundamental components of securing serverless functions in cloud environments. By defining fine-grained IAM policies and roles, developers can ensure that serverless functions have the least privilege necessary to perform their tasks, reducing the risk of unauthorized access and potential security breaches. In this article, we'll explore IAM policies and roles for serverless functions, provide code examples, and discuss best practices based on microservices design patterns for serverless applications.

1. Introduction to IAM Policies and Roles:

IAM policies and roles govern access to AWS resources and services, allowing users or entities to perform specific actions within an AWS account. IAM policies define permissions, while IAM roles define the set of permissions that an AWS service or entity can assume.

2. Least Privilege Principle:

The principle of least privilege states that users or entities should only be granted the minimum level of access necessary to perform their tasks. Applying the least privilege principle to IAM policies and roles helps minimize the potential impact of security breaches and unauthorized access.

3. IAM Policies for Serverless Functions:

IAM policies for serverless functions specify the actions that the functions are allowed to perform on AWS resources, such as invoking other services, accessing data stored in databases, or interacting with storage services.

Code Example - IAM Policy for AWS Lambda Function:

```json
{
   "Version": "2012-10-17",
   "Statement": [
      {
         "Effect": "Allow",
```

```
        "Action": [

            "dynamodb:GetItem",

            "dynamodb:PutItem",

            "logs:CreateLogGroup",

            "logs:CreateLogStream",

            "logs:PutLogEvents"

        ],

        "Resource": [

            "arn:aws:dynamodb:region:account-id:table/MyTable",

            "arn:aws:logs:region:account-id:*
}
```
```

## 4. IAM Roles for Serverless Functions:

IAM roles for serverless functions define the permissions that the functions inherit when they are executed. By assigning IAM roles to serverless functions, developers can grant permissions to access specific AWS resources without embedding credentials directly in the function code.
```

Code Example - IAM Role for AWS Lambda Function:

```json
{
  "Version": "2012-10-17",
  "Statement": [
    {
      "Effect": "Allow",
      "Action": [
        "dynamodb:GetItem",
        "dynamodb:PutItem",
        "logs:CreateLogGroup",
        "logs:CreateLogStream",
        "logs:PutLogEvents"
      ],
      "Resource": [
        "arn:aws:dynamodb:region:account-id:table/MyTable",
```

```
            "arn:aws:logs:region:account-id:*
}
```
```

### 5. Best Practices for IAM Policies and Roles:

- **Granular Permissions:** Define IAM policies with granular permissions to limit access to specific actions and resources, following the principle of least privilege.
- **Separation of Concerns:** Assign IAM roles to serverless functions based on their functional requirements, ensuring that each function only has access to the resources it needs to perform its tasks.
- **Use Managed Policies:** Leverage AWS managed policies to simplify IAM policy management and ensure compliance with security best practices.

IAM policies and roles play a critical role in securing serverless functions and ensuring the least privilege principle is followed. By defining fine-grained IAM policies and roles, developers can control access to AWS resources and services, reducing the risk of unauthorized access and potential security breaches. Incorporating best practices for IAM policies and roles based on microservices design patterns for serverless applications is essential for achieving a high level of security and compliance in modern distributed systems.
```

API Gateway Security Features: Protecting Your Application Endpoints

API Gateway serves as a central entry point for accessing backend services and APIs in microservices architectures. As such, it's crucial to implement robust security measures to protect your application endpoints from unauthorized access, data breaches, and other security threats. In this article, we'll explore the security features offered by API Gateway, provide code examples, and discuss best practices based on microservices design patterns for serverless applications.

1. Introduction to API Gateway Security:

API Gateway security involves implementing mechanisms to authenticate and authorize users, encrypt data in transit, prevent attacks such as SQL injection and cross-site scripting (XSS), and ensure the integrity and confidentiality of API requests and responses.

2. Authentication and Authorization:

API Gateway supports various authentication methods, including API keys, IAM roles, Lambda authorizers, and third-party identity providers (e.g., OAuth 2.0). These authentication mechanisms allow you to control access to your APIs and enforce security policies based on user identity, roles, or custom logic.

Code Example - API Gateway IAM Authorization:

```json
```

```
{
  "Version": "2012-10-17",
  "Statement": [
    {
      "Effect": "Allow",
      "Principal": "*",
      "Action": "execute-api:Invoke",
      "Resource": "arn:aws:execute-api:region:account-id:api-id/*/*/*"
    }
  ]
}
```

3. Encryption and Transport Layer Security (TLS):

API Gateway supports HTTPS endpoints, enabling encryption of data in transit using Transport Layer Security (TLS) to protect against eavesdropping and man-in-the-middle attacks. You can configure custom domain names and SSL certificates to ensure secure communication between clients and your APIs.

Code Example - Configuring HTTPS Endpoint:

```yaml
```

```yaml
Resources:
  MyApi:
    Type: AWS::ApiGateway::RestApi
    Properties:
      Name: MyApi
      EndpointConfiguration:
        Types:
          - REGIONAL
      BinaryMediaTypes:
        - '*/*'
      Policy:
        Version: '2012-10-17'
        Statement:
          - Effect: Allow
            Principal: "*"
            Action: "execute-api:Invoke"
            Resource:
```

```
        - "execute-api:/*/*/*"
    Tags:
      Name: MyApi
```

4. Rate Limiting and Throttling:

API Gateway allows you to implement rate limiting and throttling policies to control the number of requests clients can make to your APIs within a specific time frame. This helps prevent abuse, denial-of-service (DoS) attacks, and ensures fair usage of your resources.

Code Example - API Gateway Rate Limiting:

```json
{
  "name": "MyUsagePlan",
  "description": "Usage plan for MyApi",
  "apiStages": [
    {
      "apiId": "api-id",
      "stage": "dev"
```

```
    }
  "quota": {
    "limit": 1000,
    "period": "MONTH"
  },
  "throttle": {
    "rateLimit": 500,
    "burstLimit": 100
  }
```

5. Web Application Firewall (WAF):

API Gateway integrates with AWS WAF to protect your APIs against common web security threats, such as SQL injection, cross-site scripting (XSS), and malicious bot traffic. You can configure WAF rules and conditions to inspect and filter incoming requests based on predefined security rulesets.

Code Example - API Gateway WAF Configuration:

```json
{
```

```
"Name": "MyApiWaf",
"Description": "AWS WAF WebACL for MyApi",
"Scope": "REGIONAL",
"DefaultAction": {
  "Type": "ALLOW"
},
"Rules": [
  {
    "Name": "SQLInjectionRule",
    "Priority": 1,
    "OverrideAction": {
      "Type": "BLOCK"
    },
    "Statement": {
      "SqlInjectionMatchStatement": {
        "FieldToMatch": {
          "Type": "QUERY_STRING"
```

```
      },
        "TextTransformations": [
          {
            "Type": "URL_DECODE"
          },
        "VisibilityConfig": {
          "SampledRequestsEnabled": true,
          "CloudWatchMetricsEnabled": true,
          "MetricName": "SQLInjectionRule"
        }
      "VisibilityConfig": {
        "SampledRequestsEnabled": true,
        "CloudWatchMetricsEnabled": true,
        "MetricName": "MyApiWaf"
      }
```
```

## 6. Best Practices for API Gateway Security:
```

- **Implement Authentication:** Use appropriate authentication mechanisms, such as API keys, IAM roles, or Lambda authorizers, to verify the identity of clients accessing your APIs.
- **Enforce HTTPS:** Enable HTTPS endpoints and use SSL/TLS certificates to encrypt data in transit and protect against network-based attacks.
- **Apply Rate Limiting:** Implement rate limiting and throttling policies to control the volume of requests and prevent abuse or DoS attacks.
- **Leverage WAF:** Integrate AWS WAF to protect your APIs against common web security threats, such as SQL injection and cross-site scripting, by defining custom rulesets and conditions.
- **Monitor and Audit:** Implement logging and monitoring solutions to track API usage, monitor for suspicious activity, and detect security incidents in real-time. Utilize AWS CloudTrail and Amazon CloudWatch to capture and analyze API logs and metrics.
- **Regularly Update:** Stay informed about security vulnerabilities and updates related to API Gateway and its dependencies. Regularly update your API Gateway configurations, WAF rules, and security policies to address emerging threats and maintain a strong security posture.
- **Secure Data Handling:** Implement encryption for sensitive data at rest and in transit, using AWS Key Management Service (KMS) to manage encryption keys securely. Follow best practices for secure data handling, such as input validation, output encoding, and parameterized

queries, to prevent data breaches and injection attacks.

Securing your application endpoints with API Gateway is essential for protecting your microservices architecture from security threats and vulnerabilities. By leveraging API Gateway's security features, including authentication, authorization, encryption, rate limiting, and WAF integration, you can ensure that your APIs are protected against unauthorized access, data breaches, and other security risks.

Incorporating these security measures into your microservices design patterns for serverless applications helps you build a robust and resilient architecture that meets security and compliance requirements. By following best practices, regularly updating your security configurations, and monitoring for security incidents, you can maintain a high level of security for your serverless applications and protect your valuable data and resources.

Best Practices for Building Secure Serverless Microservices

Serverless architectures offer numerous benefits, including scalability, cost-effectiveness, and reduced operational overhead. However, ensuring the security of serverless microservices is crucial to protect sensitive data, prevent unauthorized access, and mitigate security risks. In this article, we'll explore best practices for building secure serverless microservices, provide code examples, and discuss how to implement security measures based on microservices design patterns for serverless applications.

1. Principle of Least Privilege:

The principle of least privilege states that users or components should have only the minimum level of access necessary to perform their tasks. Apply this principle to serverless microservices by defining granular IAM policies and roles, limiting permissions to only what is required for each function or service.

Code Example - IAM Policy for Lambda Function:

```json
{
  "Version": "2012-10-17",
  "Statement": [
    {
      "Effect": "Allow",
      "Action": "dynamodb:GetItem",
      "Resource": "arn:aws:dynamodb:region:account-id:table/MyTable"
    }
```

```

## 2. Secure Input Validation:

Validate and sanitize all input received by serverless functions to prevent injection attacks, such as SQL injection and cross-site scripting (XSS). Implement input validation using libraries or frameworks specific to your programming language to ensure that only valid and safe input is processed.

**Code Example - Input Validation in Python:**

```python
import re

def validate_email(email):
    if re.match(r'^[a-zA-Z0-9._%+-]+@[a-zA-Z0-9.-]+\.[a-zA-Z]{2,}$', email):
        return True
    return False
```

3. Implement Encryption:

Encrypt sensitive data at rest and in transit to protect it from unauthorized access and interception. Use encryption mechanisms provided by cloud providers, such as AWS Key Management Service (KMS), to
```

encrypt data stored in databases or transmitted between services.

Code Example - Encrypting Data in Node.js:

```javascript
const AWS = require('aws-sdk');

const kms = new AWS.KMS();

const encryptData = async (data) => {

  const params = { KeyId: 'my-key-id', Plaintext: data };

  const encryptedData = await kms.encrypt(params).promise();

  return encryptedData.CiphertextBlob;

};
```

4. Secure Communication:

Ensure that communication between serverless functions and external services is secure by using HTTPS endpoints, SSL/TLS encryption, and signed API requests. Validate SSL certificates and implement certificate pinning to prevent man-in-the-middle attacks.

Code Example - HTTPS Endpoint Configuration:

```yaml
Resources:
  MyApi:
    Type: AWS::ApiGateway::RestApi
    Properties:
      Name: MyApi
      EndpointConfiguration:
        Types:
          - REGIONAL
      Policy:
        Version: '2012-10-17'
        Statement:
          - Effect: Allow
            Principal: "*"
            Action: "execute-api:Invoke"
            Resource: "execute-api:/*/*/*"
      Tags:
```

    Name: MyApi

```

### 5. Implement Logging and Monitoring:

Enable logging and monitoring for serverless functions to track and analyze activity, detect anomalies, and respond to security incidents in real-time. Utilize cloud-native logging and monitoring services, such as Amazon CloudWatch, to capture and analyze logs and metrics.

### Code Example - Logging in Python:

```python
import logging

def lambda_handler(event, context):
    logger = logging.getLogger()
    logger.setLevel(logging.INFO)
    logger.info('Function executed successfully')
```

6. Regularly Update Dependencies:

Keep dependencies, libraries, and frameworks used by serverless functions up-to-date to address security vulnerabilities and patch known vulnerabilities. Use
```

automated tools or services to monitor for security advisories and apply updates promptly.

Building secure serverless microservices requires a proactive approach to identify and mitigate security risks at every stage of development and deployment. By following best practices such as implementing the principle of least privilege, securing input validation, encrypting data, ensuring secure communication, implementing logging and monitoring, and regularly updating dependencies, you can build resilient and secure serverless microservices architectures.

Incorporating these security measures into your microservices design patterns for serverless applications helps you protect sensitive data, maintain compliance with security regulations, and mitigate the risk of security breaches. By prioritizing security from the outset and adopting a security-first mindset, you can build serverless microservices that are robust, reliable, and resilient against emerging security threats.

Chapter 10

The Importance of Testing Microservices: Unit Testing, Integration Testing, and End-to-End Testing

Testing microservices in serverless applications is crucial for ensuring reliability, scalability, and maintainability. In this article, we'll delve into the importance of three key types of testing: unit testing, integration testing, and end-to-end testing, within the context of microservices architecture for serverless applications.

Introduction to Microservices in Serverless Applications

Serverless architecture has gained popularity due to its scalability, cost-effectiveness, and ease of deployment. In this paradigm, applications are composed of loosely coupled, independently deployable microservices. Each microservice is responsible for a specific business function and communicates with other services through APIs.

The Importance of Testing Microservices

Unit Testing

Unit testing is the foundation of any testing strategy. It involves testing individual units or components of a microservice in isolation. For serverless applications, unit tests ensure that each function behaves as expected, independent of its environment.

Let's consider an example of a serverless function written in Node.js:

```javascript
// function.js

exports.handler = async (event) => {

  const { num1, num2 } = event;

  const sum = num1 + num2;

  return { result: sum };

};
```

A corresponding unit test for this function using a testing framework like Jest could look like this:

```javascript
// function.test.js

const { handler } = require('./function');

test('adds 1 + 2 to equal 3', async () => {

  const event = { num1: 1, num2: 2 };
```

```javascript
    const response = await handler(event);

    expect(response.result).toBe(3);
});
```

Unit tests ensure that each function behaves correctly under various inputs and conditions, helping to catch bugs early in the development process.

Integration Testing

Integration testing verifies the interaction between different microservices. In a serverless environment, integration tests validate that services communicate correctly and handle data exchange appropriately.

Consider a scenario where our previous function interacts with another service to perform additional computation:

```javascript
// function.js

const externalService = require('./externalService');

exports.handler = async (event) => {
  const { num1, num2 } = event;

  const sum = num1 + num2;
```

```javascript
  const externalResult = await externalService.calculate(num1, num2);

  return { result: sum, externalResult };
};
```

An integration test for this scenario ensures that the function interacts correctly with the external service:

```javascript
// integration.test.js

const { handler } = require('./function');

const externalService = require('./externalService');

jest.mock('./externalService');

test('integrates with external service correctly', async () => {

  externalService.calculate.mockResolvedValue(5);

  const event = { num1: 1, num2: 2 };

  const response = await handler(event);

  expect(response.result).toBe(3);

  expect(response.externalResult).toBe(5);
```

});
```

Integration tests validate that microservices work together seamlessly, identifying any compatibility issues or unexpected behavior.

### End-to-End Testing

End-to-end (E2E) testing evaluates the entire application workflow from start to finish. In a serverless context, E2E tests simulate real-world user interactions and verify that the application functions correctly as a whole.

Consider an E2E test for our serverless application that sends a request to an API gateway endpoint:

```javascript
// e2e.test.js

const axios = require('axios');

const API_URL = 'https://example.com/api';

test('performs end-to-end testing successfully', async () => {

  const response = await axios.post(API_URL, { num1: 1, num2: 2 });

  expect(response.status).toBe(200);

expect(response.data.result).toBe(3);

});

```

This test sends a request to the API gateway endpoint, mimicking a real user interaction, and asserts that the response meets the expected criteria.

Testing microservices in serverless applications is essential for ensuring reliability, scalability, and maintainability. Unit testing, integration testing, and end-to-end testing play complementary roles in validating the functionality and interaction of microservices.

By incorporating these testing strategies into the development lifecycle, teams can identify and address issues early, leading to higher-quality software and improved user satisfaction.

Unit Testing Lambda Functions: Ensuring Individual Function Functionality

Unit testing Lambda functions is crucial for ensuring the functionality and reliability of individual microservices within a serverless application. In this article, we'll explore the importance of unit testing Lambda functions, discuss best practices, and provide examples using Node.js within the context of microservices design patterns for serverless applications.
```

Introduction to Unit Testing Lambda Functions

Lambda functions are at the core of serverless architecture, responsible for handling specific tasks or business logic within a serverless application. Unit testing Lambda functions involves testing the functionality of each function in isolation, independent of its environment or external dependencies. This ensures that each function behaves as expected and produces the desired output given different inputs.

Importance of Unit Testing Lambda Functions

1. Early Bug Detection:

Unit tests allow developers to identify and fix bugs early in the development process, reducing the likelihood of issues in production.

2. Improved Code Quality:

Writing unit tests encourages writing modular, testable code, leading to better code quality and maintainability.

3. Faster Development Cycle:

Automated unit tests provide rapid feedback, allowing developers to iterate quickly and confidently, speeding up the development cycle.

Best Practices for Unit Testing Lambda Functions

1. Keep Functions Small and Single-Purpose:

Divide Lambda functions into smaller, single-purpose units to make them easier to test and maintain.

2. Mock External Dependencies:

Use mocking frameworks to simulate external dependencies such as database connections or API calls, ensuring that tests remain isolated and deterministic.

3. Test Edge Cases:

Write tests to cover edge cases and boundary conditions to ensure that functions handle unexpected inputs gracefully.

4. Automate Testing:

Integrate unit tests into the continuous integration (CI) pipeline to automate testing and ensure that all code changes are thoroughly validated.

Example: Unit Testing Lambda Functions in Node.js

Let's consider a simple Lambda function written in Node.js that calculates the sum of two numbers:

```javascript
// sumFunction.js

exports.handler = async (event) => {
  const { num1, num2 } = event;
```

```
  const sum = num1 + num2;
  return { result: sum };
};
```

To unit test this Lambda function, we'll use the Jest testing framework and create a corresponding test file:

```javascript
// sumFunction.test.js
const { handler } = require('./sumFunction');
describe('Lambda Function: Sum', () => {
  test('adds 1 + 2 to equal 3', async () => {
    const event = { num1: 1, num2: 2 };
    const result = await handler(event);
    expect(result.result).toBe(3);
  });
  test('adds -1 + 1 to equal 0', async () => {
    const event = { num1: -1, num2: 1 };
    const result = await handler(event);
```

```
    expect(result.result).toBe(0);

  });

  test('handles large numbers correctly', async () => {

    const event = { num1: 1000000000, num2: 2000000000 };

    const result = await handler(event);

    expect(result.result).toBe(3000000000);

  });

```

In this test suite, we've covered basic scenarios such as adding positive and negative numbers, as well as testing with large numbers to ensure that the function behaves correctly in various scenarios.

Unit testing Lambda functions is essential for ensuring the functionality and reliability of individual microservices within a serverless application. By following best practices and writing comprehensive unit tests, developers can detect bugs early, improve code quality, and accelerate the development cycle. Automated unit testing, coupled with continuous integration, enables teams to build and maintain robust serverless applications with confidence.

Integration Testing Microservices: Verifying Communication and Data Flow

Integration testing microservices is vital for verifying communication and data flow between different components within a serverless application. In this article, we'll explore the importance of integration testing, discuss key considerations, and provide examples using microservices design patterns for serverless applications.

Introduction to Integration Testing Microservices

Microservices architecture decomposes applications into smaller, independently deployable services, each responsible for a specific business function. Integration testing ensures that these services interact correctly with each other, exchange data seamlessly, and maintain overall system functionality.

Importance of Integration Testing

1. End-to-End Functionality:

Integration tests verify the end-to-end functionality of a system, ensuring that all microservices work together as expected to fulfill business requirements.

2. Data Consistency:

Testing data flow between microservices helps maintain data consistency and integrity across the application, preventing issues such as data loss or corruption.

3. Fault Detection:

Integration tests uncover integration errors, such as incorrect API endpoints or incompatible data formats, enabling developers to detect and resolve issues early in the development lifecycle.

Key Considerations for Integration Testing

1. Mocking External Dependencies:

Mocking frameworks simulate external dependencies, such as databases or third-party APIs, allowing integration tests to run independently and deterministically without relying on external resources.

2. Test Data Management:

Managing test data ensures that integration tests have access to consistent and relevant data, facilitating accurate validation of data flow between microservices.

3. Test Environment Isolation:

Isolating test environments from production environments prevents interference and ensures that integration tests do not impact live systems or data.

Example: Integration Testing Microservices in a Serverless Application

Let's consider a serverless application composed of two microservices: an authentication service and a user service. The authentication service verifies user credentials and generates access tokens, while the user service manages user data.

```javascript
// authenticationService.js

exports.authenticate = async (username, password) => {

  // Authentication logic

};

exports.generateAccessToken = async (userId) => {

  // Token generation logic

};
```

```javascript
// userService.js

exports.getUserById = async (userId) => {

  // Retrieve user data from database

};

exports.updateUser = async (userId, userData) => {

  // Update user data in the database

};
```

To perform integration testing, we'll verify that the authentication service correctly generates an access token and that the user service can retrieve and update user data using the access token.

```javascript
// integrationTest.js

const authenticationService = require('./authenticationService');

const userService = require('./userService');

describe('Integration Testing: Authentication and User Services', () => {

  let accessToken;

  beforeAll(async () => {

    // Mock authentication

    accessToken = await authenticationService.generateAccessToken('userId123');

  test('should authenticate user and generate access token', async () => {

    const isAuthenticated = await authenticationService.authenticate('username', 'password');
```

```
    expect(isAuthenticated).toBeTruthy();

    expect(accessToken).toBeDefined();
  });

  test('should retrieve user data using access token', async () => {
    const userData = await userService.getUserById('userId123', accessToken);

    expect(userData).toEqual(expect.objectContaining({ id: 'userId123' }));
  });

  test('should update user data using access token', async () => {
    const updatedUserData = { name: 'Updated Name' };

    const updatedUser = await userService.updateUser('userId123', updatedUserData, accessToken);

    expect(updatedUser).toEqual(expect.objectContaining({ name: 'Updated Name' }));
  });
```
```
```

In this integration test suite, we've simulated the authentication process by generating an access token using the authentication service. We then test the user service's ability to retrieve and update user data using the generated access token. Mocking external dependencies ensures that the tests remain isolated and deterministic.

Integration testing microservices is essential for verifying communication and data flow within a serverless application. By testing interactions between microservices, developers can ensure end-to-end functionality, maintain data consistency, and detect integration errors early in the development process. Following key considerations and best practices enables teams to build and maintain robust serverless applications with confidence.

Testing Tools and Frameworks for Serverless Applications

Testing serverless applications, especially those built using microservices design patterns, requires a robust set of tools and frameworks to ensure reliability, scalability, and maintainability. In this article, we'll explore some of the most popular testing tools and frameworks for serverless applications, along with code examples demonstrating their usage within the context of microservices design patterns.

Introduction to Testing Tools for Serverless Applications

Testing serverless applications involves various types of testing, including unit testing, integration testing, end-to-end testing, and performance testing. Each type of testing requires specialized tools and frameworks to effectively validate different aspects of the application's functionality.

1. Unit Testing Tools

- **Jest**

Jest is a popular JavaScript testing framework that provides a simple and intuitive API for writing unit tests. It supports features like test runners, assertions, mocking, and code coverage analysis.

Example usage of Jest for unit testing a Lambda function:

```javascript
// sumFunction.test.js

const { handler } = require('./sumFunction');

test('adds 1 + 2 to equal 3', async () => {
  const event = { num1: 1, num2: 2 };
  const result = await handler(event);
  expect(result.result).toBe(3);
});
```

```

- **Mocha**

Mocha is another widely-used JavaScript testing framework that offers support for asynchronous testing, multiple assertion libraries, and various test reporters.

**Example usage of Mocha for unit testing a Lambda function:**

```javascript

// sumFunction.test.js

const { handler } = require('./sumFunction');

const assert = require('assert');

describe('Sum Function', () => {

  it('should add 1 + 2 to equal 3', async () => {

    const event = { num1: 1, num2: 2 };

    const result = await handler(event);

    assert.strictEqual(result.result, 3);

  });

});

```

2. Integration Testing Tools
```

- **Supertest**

Supertest is a lightweight library for testing HTTP servers, making it ideal for integration testing serverless applications that expose RESTful APIs.

Example usage of Supertest for integration testing an API endpoint:

```javascript
// integration.test.js

const request = require('supertest');

const app = require('./app'); // Express app

describe('GET /api/users', () => {
  it('responds with JSON', (done) => {
    request(app)
      .get('/api/users')
      .expect('Content-Type', /json/)
      .expect(200, done);
  });
});
```

- **Chai HTTP**

Chai HTTP is an HTTP plugin for the Chai assertion library, providing a fluent interface for making HTTP requests and asserting response properties.

Example usage of Chai HTTP for integration testing an API endpoint:

```javascript
// integration.test.js

const chai = require('chai');

const chaiHttp = require('chai-http');

const app = require('./app'); // Express app

chai.use(chaiHttp);

describe('GET /api/users', () => {
  it('responds with JSON', (done) => {
    chai.request(app)
      .get('/api/users')
      .end((err, res) => {
        chai.expect(res).to.have.status(200);
        chai.expect(res).to.be.json;
        done();
```

```
    });
```

3. End-to-End Testing Tools

- **<u>Cypress</u>**

Cypress is a modern end-to-end testing framework designed specifically for web applications. It provides a comprehensive set of tools for writing, running, and debugging tests in a real browser environment.

Example usage of Cypress for end-to-end testing a web application:

```javascript
// e2e.spec.js
describe('End-to-End Testing', () => {
  it('should load the homepage', () => {
    cy.visit('/');
    cy.contains('Welcome to My App');
  });
  it('should navigate to the login page', () => {
    cy.visit('/');
```

```
    cy.get('a[href="/login"]').click();

    cy.url().should('include', '/login');

  });
```
```

Testing serverless applications, especially those built using microservices design patterns, requires a diverse set of tools and frameworks to cover different types of testing scenarios. Unit testing tools like Jest and Mocha are essential for validating individual components, while integration testing tools like Supertest and Chai HTTP help verify interactions between microservices. For end-to-end testing, Cypress provides a powerful solution for testing the entire application workflow in a real browser environment. By leveraging these testing tools and frameworks, developers can ensure the reliability, scalability, and maintainability of their serverless applications.
```

Chapter 11

Why Monitoring is Crucial for Serverless Applications

Serverless architecture has revolutionized the way applications are built and deployed, offering scalability, cost efficiency, and reduced operational overhead. However, with the distributed nature of serverless applications, monitoring becomes even more critical to ensure reliability, performance, and security. In this article, we'll explore why monitoring is crucial for serverless applications, focusing on microservices design patterns.

1. Scalability and Resource Optimization: Serverless platforms automatically scale resources based on demand, allowing applications to handle varying workloads efficiently. However, without proper monitoring, it's challenging to optimize resource allocation and identify potential bottlenecks.

Consider a microservices-based serverless application where each function performs a specific task. Monitoring metrics such as invocation count, execution duration, and resource utilization provide insights into the performance of individual functions. By analyzing these metrics, developers can optimize resource allocation, adjust concurrency limits, and fine-tune function configurations to ensure optimal scalability and cost efficiency.

```python
# Example code for monitoring invocation count and execution duration of a serverless function

import time

def my_function(event, context):
    start_time = time.time()

    # Function logic

    end_time = time.time()

    execution_duration = end_time - start_time

    # Log metrics

    log_metrics(invocation_count=1, execution_duration=execution_duration)

    return "Success"
```

2. Fault Tolerance and Error Handling: In a microservices architecture, failures can occur at any level, from individual functions to external service dependencies. Monitoring helps in detecting and responding to errors promptly, ensuring high availability and fault tolerance.

By monitoring error rates, latency, and error messages, developers can identify patterns and root causes of failures. Automated alerting systems can notify operators of critical issues, enabling them to take corrective actions, such as restarting failed functions or rolling back deployments.

```python
# Example code for logging errors in a serverless function

def my_function(event, context):
    try:
        # Function logic
        return "Success"
    except Exception as e:
        # Log error
        log_error(e)
        return "Error"
```

3. Performance Optimization: Performance optimization is essential for delivering a seamless user experience and meeting service level agreements

(SLAs). Monitoring helps in identifying performance bottlenecks, inefficient code, and resource constraints.

By analyzing metrics such as cold start times, memory usage, and invocation concurrency, developers can optimize function performance and reduce latency. Techniques such as pre-warming, caching, and asynchronous processing can be employed based on insights gained from monitoring data.

```python
# Example code for monitoring cold start times of a serverless function

def my_function(event, context):
    start_time = time.time()
    # Function logic
    end_time = time.time()
    cold_start_time = end_time - start_time
    # Log cold start time
    log_metric(cold_start_time=cold_start_time)
    return "Success"
```

4. Security and Compliance: Security is a top priority for any application, especially in distributed environments like serverless architectures. Monitoring helps in detecting and mitigating security threats, vulnerabilities, and compliance violations.

By monitoring access logs, API calls, and system activity, developers can identify unauthorized access attempts, anomalous behavior, and potential security breaches. Integrating with security information and event management (SIEM) systems enables real-time threat detection and response.

```python
# Example code for logging access to sensitive resources in a serverless function

def my_function(event, context):
    # Check access permissions
    if is_authorized(event):
        # Access sensitive resource
        log_access(event)
        return "Success"
    else:
        # Log unauthorized access attempt
```

```
        log_security_event(event, "Unauthorized access")

        return "Unauthorized"
```

Monitoring is essential for ensuring the reliability, performance, and security of serverless applications, particularly when adopting microservices design patterns. By continuously monitoring key metrics and logs, developers can optimize resource usage, enhance fault tolerance, improve performance, and strengthen security posture. Implementing a robust monitoring strategy is crucial for unlocking the full potential of serverless architecture and delivering a seamless user experience.

CloudWatch Logs and Metrics for Monitoring Lambda Functions

Lambda functions are the backbone of serverless applications, providing scalable and cost-effective compute resources. Monitoring Lambda functions is crucial for ensuring reliability, performance, and security. In this article, we'll explore how to utilize CloudWatch Logs and Metrics effectively to monitor Lambda functions in a microservices architecture.

1. Setting Up CloudWatch Logs for Lambda Functions:

CloudWatch Logs allows you to monitor, store, and analyze logs generated by Lambda functions. Setting up

CloudWatch Logs for Lambda functions is essential for troubleshooting, performance analysis, and compliance auditing.

To enable CloudWatch Logs for a Lambda function, you can configure it through the AWS Management Console or using AWS CloudFormation templates.

```yaml
Resources:
  MyLambdaFunction:
    Type: AWS::Lambda::Function
    Properties:
      FunctionName: my-lambda-function
      Handler: index.handler
      Role: arn:aws:iam::123456789012:role/lambda-role
      Runtime: nodejs14.x
      Timeout: 30
      Environment:
        Variables:
          ENVIRONMENT: production
```

```
      TracingConfig:
        Mode: Active
      Events:
        MyEvent:
          Type: ApiGatewayHttpApi
          Properties:
            Path: /my-path
            Method: GET
      LogGroupName: /aws/lambda/my-lambda-function
```

Once enabled, Lambda function logs are automatically streamed to CloudWatch Logs, where you can search, filter, and analyze them using CloudWatch Logs Insights.

2. Monitoring Lambda Function Metrics with CloudWatch:

CloudWatch Metrics provide insights into the performance and behavior of Lambda functions, allowing you to track key metrics such as invocation count, duration, error rate, and concurrency.

```python
```

```python
import boto3

cloudwatch = boto3.client('cloudwatch')

def put_metric_data(metric_name, value, dimensions):
    response = cloudwatch.put_metric_data(
        Namespace='AWS/Lambda',
        MetricData=[
            {
                'MetricName': metric_name,
                'Dimensions': dimensions,
                'Value': value,
                'Unit': 'Count'
            },
    print(response)

# Example code for publishing custom metrics for a Lambda function

def my_lambda_function(event, context):
    # Function logic
    # Publish custom metrics
```

    put_metric_data('CustomMetric', 1, [{'Name': 'FunctionName', 'Value': context.function_name}])

    return "Success"

```

By creating custom CloudWatch Metrics and publishing them from Lambda functions, you can track application-specific performance indicators and business metrics.

## 3. Analyzing Lambda Function Performance with CloudWatch Logs Insights:

CloudWatch Logs Insights is a powerful tool for analyzing and visualizing log data from Lambda functions. With CloudWatch Logs Insights, you can run ad-hoc queries, create dashboards, and set up alarms based on log patterns and metrics.

```sql
# Example CloudWatch Logs Insights query to analyze Lambda function logs

fields @timestamp, @message

| filter @message like /ERROR/

| stats count(*) as error_count by bin(1h)

| sort @timestamp desc

| limit 20

```

By writing SQL-like queries in CloudWatch Logs Insights, you can identify errors, anomalies, and performance issues in Lambda function logs, enabling proactive monitoring and troubleshooting.

4. Implementing Distributed Tracing with AWS X-Ray:

AWS X-Ray is a distributed tracing service that helps you analyze and debug microservices architectures, including Lambda functions. By instrumenting Lambda functions with X-Ray, you can trace requests as they traverse through different components of your application.

```python
import aws_xray_sdk.core

# Initialize X-Ray SDK
aws_xray_sdk.core.patch_all()

# Example code for instrumenting Lambda function with X-Ray
def my_lambda_function(event, context):
    # Function logic
    # Generate trace segment
```
```

```
with aws_xray_sdk.core.patch('lambda'):

    # Function logic

    return "Success"
```

By integrating X-Ray with Lambda functions, you can gain insights into request latency, dependencies, and error rates, facilitating performance optimization and troubleshooting.

Monitoring Lambda functions is essential for ensuring the reliability, performance, and security of serverless applications, especially in microservices architectures. By leveraging CloudWatch Logs and Metrics, along with tools like CloudWatch Logs Insights and AWS X-Ray, developers can gain visibility into the behavior and performance of Lambda functions, enabling proactive monitoring, troubleshooting, and optimization. Implementing a robust monitoring strategy is crucial for delivering a seamless user experience and maintaining the health of serverless applications.

Application Performance Monitoring (APM) Tools for Microservices

In the context of modern software development, microservices architecture has gained significant traction due to its scalability, flexibility, and resilience. Microservices break down applications into smaller, loosely coupled services, which can be independently developed, deployed, and scaled.

However, the distributed nature of microservices brings challenges in terms of monitoring and troubleshooting. This is where Application Performance Monitoring (APM) tools come into play. APM tools provide insights into the performance and health of microservices, helping developers and operators to detect, diagnose, and resolve issues quickly.

For serverless applications, which leverage cloud services to abstract away infrastructure management, APM becomes even more crucial. As serverless applications are inherently distributed and event-driven, traditional monitoring approaches may not suffice.

Key Features of APM Tools for Microservices

1. Distributed Tracing: APM tools should support distributed tracing to track requests as they traverse through multiple microservices. This helps in understanding the flow of requests and identifying latency bottlenecks.

2. Metrics Collection: Monitoring metrics such as CPU utilization, memory usage, and request throughput across microservices is essential for detecting anomalies and optimizing performance.

3. Log Aggregation: Centralized log management enables developers to correlate logs from different microservices, aiding in troubleshooting and root cause analysis.

4. Alerting and Notification: APM tools should support customizable alerts and notifications based on predefined thresholds or anomalies, allowing proactive issue resolution.

5. Integration with Cloud Providers: Seamless integration with cloud providers' monitoring services, such as AWS CloudWatch or Azure Monitor, facilitates monitoring of serverless functions and infrastructure.

APM Tools for Microservices: Code Examples

Let's explore how to integrate APM tools into a serverless microservices architecture using code examples. We'll focus on AWS Lambda functions and AWS X-Ray for distributed tracing.

Setting up AWS X-Ray

```python
import boto3

from aws_xray_sdk.core import xray_recorder

from aws_xray_sdk.core import patch_all

# Patching libraries to enable X-Ray tracing

patch_all()
```

```
# Initialize AWS SDK
client = boto3.client('lambda')
# Define Lambda function handler
def lambda_handler(event, context):
    # Start a segment for X-Ray tracing
    with xray_recorder.in_segment('MyLambdaFunction'):
        # Your function logic here
        return 'Hello from Lambda!'
```

Configuring X-Ray Sampling Rules

```json
{
  "Version": 1,
  "Rules": [
    {
      "Description": "Default rule",
      "ServiceName": "*",
```

```
    "Host": "*",

    "HTTPMethod": "*",

    "URLPath": "*",

    "FixedRate": 0.1

}
...
```

Analyzing Traces in AWS X-Ray Console

Once the Lambda function is invoked, traces will be recorded in AWS X-Ray. Developers can analyze these traces in the X-Ray console to gain insights into the performance of individual functions and their interactions.

Application Performance Monitoring (APM) tools play a crucial role in ensuring the reliability and efficiency of microservices-based serverless applications. By leveraging tools like AWS X-Ray and integrating them into the development workflow, developers can gain visibility into the performance of their applications, detect issues early, and optimize for better user experience.

Remember, monitoring is not a one-time task but an ongoing process. Continuously monitor and refine your monitoring strategy to adapt to changing requirements and scale effectively.

Best Practices for Effective Monitoring and Debugging of Serverless Applications

Monitoring and debugging serverless applications in a microservices architecture require a strategic approach to ensure optimal performance and reliability. Let's delve into best practices for effective monitoring and debugging, incorporating code examples and microservices design patterns:

1. Implement Comprehensive Logging:

- Utilize structured logging to capture relevant information such as timestamps, request IDs, and function names.
- Log both application-level and system-level events to gain insights into the entire application stack.

- **Example (Node.js):**

```javascript
const logger = require('structured-logger');

module.exports.handler = async (event, context) => {

    logger.info('Processing request', { event, context });

    // Business logic

};
```

```

## 2. Leverage Distributed Tracing:

- Implement tracing mechanisms to trace requests across multiple serverless functions and microservices.
- Use correlation IDs to link related logs and traces together.

- **Example (AWS X-Ray):**

```javascript

const AWSXRay = require('aws-xray-sdk-core');

const AWS = AWSXRay.captureAWS(require('aws-sdk'));

AWSXRay.captureHTTPsGlobal(require('http'));

```

3. Set Up Monitoring Alarms:

- Configure alarms based on metrics like error rates, latency, and resource utilization to proactively detect issues.
- Utilize cloud provider's monitoring services like AWS CloudWatch or Azure Monitor.

- **Example (AWS CloudWatch Alarm):**

```yaml

```
AWSTemplateFormatVersion: '2010-09-09'
Resources:
  HighErrorRateAlarm:
    Type: 'AWS::CloudWatch::Alarm'
    Properties:
      AlarmDescription: 'Alarm on high error rate'
      Namespace: 'AWS/Lambda'
      MetricName: 'Errors'
      Dimensions:
        - Name: 'FunctionName'
          Value: 'YourLambdaFunctionName'
      Statistic: 'Sum'
      Period: 60
      EvaluationPeriods: 1
      Threshold: 5
      ComparisonOperator: 'GreaterThanThreshold'
```

4. Implement Circuit Breaker Pattern:

- Use circuit breakers to prevent cascading failures by temporarily halting requests to a failing microservice.
- Configure timeouts and thresholds for circuit breaker transitions.

- **Example (Node.js with `circuit-breaker-js`):**

```javascript
const CircuitBreaker = require('circuit-breaker-js');

const circuit = new CircuitBreaker(yourFunction, {
    timeoutDuration: 3000,
    volumeThreshold: 5,
    errorThreshold: 50
});

async function yourFunction() {
    // Perform microservice call
}
```

5. Implement Retry Mechanisms:

- Handle transient failures by implementing retry logic with exponential backoff.
- Use libraries like `aws-sdk` for built-in retry functionality.

- **Example (AWS SDK for JavaScript):**

```javascript
const AWS = require('aws-sdk');
const lambda = new AWS.Lambda();
const params = {
    FunctionName: 'YourFunctionName',
    InvocationType: 'RequestResponse',
    Payload: JSON.stringify(payload)
};
lambda.invoke(params, function(err, data) {
    if (err) {
        console.error('Error invoking function:', err);
    } else {
        console.log('Function response:', data.Payload);
    }
});
```

```

## 6. Implement Health Checks:

- Implement health checks for serverless functions and microservices to monitor their availability.
- Health checks can be simple HTTP endpoints or custom checks based on business logic.

- **Example (Node.js with Express):**

```javascript

const express = require('express');

const app = express();

app.get('/health', (req, res) => {

  res.status(200).send('OK');

});

const server = app.listen(3000, () => {

  console.log('Server is running on port 3000');

});
```

7. Use Canary Deployments:
```

- Implement canary deployments to gradually roll out updates and monitor their impact before full deployment.
- Route a small percentage of traffic to the new version and gradually increase it based on performance metrics.

Example (AWS Lambda with AWS CodeDeploy):

- Define deployment configurations in AWS CodeDeploy to specify traffic shifting rules.

8. Automate Testing and Deployment:

- Implement continuous integration and continuous deployment (CI/CD) pipelines to automate testing and deployment processes.
- Incorporate unit tests, integration tests, and end-to-end tests into your pipeline.

Example (AWS CodePipeline with AWS CodeBuild and AWS CodeDeploy):

- Configure stages for build, test, and deploy actions in AWS CodePipeline.

9. Monitor Cold Start Performance:

- Monitor and optimize cold start performance of serverless functions to minimize latency.
- Consider using provisioned concurrency to reduce cold start times for critical functions.

Example (AWS Lambda Provisioned Concurrency):

- Configure provisioned concurrency settings in AWS Lambda console or via AWS SDK.

10. Implement Security Monitoring:

- Monitor for security events and anomalies by integrating with security information and event management (SIEM) systems.
- Monitor for unauthorized access, abnormal behavior, and potential security vulnerabilities.

Example (AWS CloudTrail with AWS Config):

- Enable AWS CloudTrail logging and configure AWS Config rules to detect security policy violations.

By incorporating these best practices into your serverless application development and operations, you can effectively monitor and debug your microservices architecture, ensuring high availability, reliability, and performance. Remember to continuously review and optimize your monitoring and debugging strategies to adapt to evolving application requirements and environments.

Chapter 12

Emerging Trends and Advancements in Serverless Technologies

Emerging trends and advancements in serverless technologies are reshaping the way developers build and deploy applications, especially in the context of microservices architecture. Let's explore some of these trends and advancements along with code examples and microservices design patterns:

1. Increased Adoption of Kubernetes with Serverless:

- Combining Kubernetes with serverless technologies provides a powerful platform for managing containerized workloads.
- Kubernetes-based serverless frameworks like Knative and Kubeless enable developers to deploy and scale functions seamlessly.

Example (Knative):

- Define a Knative service using Kubernetes YAML manifests to deploy serverless functions.

2. Integration of Machine Learning with Serverless:

- Serverless platforms are increasingly supporting machine learning workloads, enabling developers to build and deploy AI-powered applications.

331

- Serverless machine learning frameworks like AWS Lambda with Amazon SageMaker and TensorFlow Serving with Kubernetes facilitate model inference at scale.

Example (AWS Lambda with Amazon SageMaker):

- Invoke SageMaker endpoints from AWS Lambda functions to perform real-time predictions.

3. Event-Driven Architectures and Event Sourcing:

- Event-driven architectures (EDA) are becoming more prevalent, leveraging serverless technologies for event processing and handling.
- Event sourcing patterns enable capturing and persisting domain events for building event-driven systems.

Example (AWS EventBridge):

- Use AWS EventBridge to route events between different services and systems in a serverless architecture.

4. Serverless GraphQL APIs:

- GraphQL is gaining popularity for building APIs due to its flexibility and efficiency.
- Serverless platforms like AWS AppSync and Azure Functions with GraphQL enable developers to build scalable GraphQL APIs without managing servers.

Example (AWS AppSync):

- Define GraphQL schema and resolvers using AWS AppSync console or GraphQL SDL.

5. Edge Computing with Serverless:

- Serverless computing at the edge brings compute resources closer to end-users, reducing latency and improving performance.
- Edge computing platforms like AWS Lambda@Edge and Cloudflare Workers enable running serverless functions at CDN edge locations.

Example (AWS Lambda@Edge):

- Write Lambda functions to intercept and modify requests and responses at CloudFront edge locations.

6. Hybrid Cloud Deployments:

- Hybrid cloud deployments combine on-premises infrastructure with public cloud services, offering flexibility and scalability.
- Serverless frameworks like Google Cloud Run and AWS Outposts enable running serverless workloads on-premises and in the cloud.

Example (Google Cloud Run):

- Deploy containerized serverless applications to Google Cloud Run on Anthos clusters running on-premises.

7. Container Orchestration for Serverless Workloads:

- Container orchestration platforms like AWS ECS and Google Kubernetes Engine (GKE) support running serverless workloads in containers.
- Kubernetes-based serverless frameworks like OpenFaaS and Kubeless enable deploying and scaling functions as containers.

Example (OpenFaaS):

- Deploy serverless functions as Docker containers to an OpenFaaS cluster managed by Kubernetes.

8. Distributed Tracing and Observability:

- Distributed tracing tools like Jaeger and Zipkin are becoming essential for monitoring and debugging serverless applications.
- Observability platforms like AWS X-Ray and Google Cloud Monitoring provide insights into the performance and behavior of serverless functions.

Example (AWS X-Ray):

- Instrument Lambda functions with AWS X-Ray SDK to trace requests across distributed systems.

9. Serverless DevOps and CI/CD Pipelines:

- Serverless DevOps practices emphasize automation, collaboration, and continuous delivery for serverless applications.
- CI/CD pipelines tailored for serverless workflows enable automated testing, deployment, and monitoring.

Example (AWS CodePipeline with AWS CodeBuild and AWS CodeDeploy):

- Configure CI/CD pipeline stages for building, testing, and deploying serverless applications.

10. Serverless Security and Compliance:

- Serverless security solutions address challenges such as data protection, access control, and compliance requirements.
- Tools like AWS Lambda Layers and Azure Key Vault provide mechanisms for securing serverless applications and managing secrets.

Example (Azure Key Vault):

- Store sensitive information like API keys and database credentials securely in Azure Key Vault and access them from serverless functions.

These emerging trends and advancements in serverless technologies are shaping the future of application development, enabling developers to build scalable, resilient, and cost-effective solutions using microservices design patterns. By staying abreast of these trends and leveraging the appropriate tools and frameworks, developers can harness the full potential of serverless computing for their applications.

The Future of Microservices Architecture: Continuous Innovation and Flexibility

The future of microservices architecture is centered around continuous innovation and flexibility, driven by advancements in serverless technologies and cloud-native development practices. Let's explore how microservices architecture will continue to evolve to meet the demands of modern application development, with code examples and a focus on serverless design patterns:

1. Serverless Microservices:

- Serverless computing is reshaping microservices architecture by providing a more efficient and cost-effective way to build and deploy services.
- Serverless microservices leverage cloud providers' managed services, enabling developers to focus on business logic rather than infrastructure management.

Example (AWS Lambda):

- Define individual microservices as Lambda functions, each responsible for a specific domain or functionality.

```javascript
// Example AWS Lambda function
exports.handler = async (event) => {
  // Business logic
  return {
    statusCode: 200,
    body: JSON.stringify({ message: 'Hello from Lambda!' }),
  };
};
```

2. Event-Driven Architecture (EDA):

- Event-driven architecture is gaining prominence in microservices design, facilitating loose coupling and scalability.
- Microservices communicate via events, enabling asynchronous and decoupled interactions between components.

Example (AWS EventBridge):

- Define event rules to trigger Lambda functions in response to events from various sources.

```javascript
```

```
// Example AWS Lambda function triggered by EventBridge

exports.handler = async (event) => {

  // Process event

  console.log('Received event:', JSON.stringify(event, null, 2));

};
```

3. Containerization and Kubernetes:

- Containers and Kubernetes continue to play a vital role in microservices architecture, providing portability and scalability.
- Kubernetes orchestrates containerized microservices, offering features like service discovery, scaling, and rolling updates.

Example (Kubernetes Deployment):

- Define Kubernetes deployment manifests for deploying containerized microservices.

```yaml
apiVersion: apps/v1

kind: Deployment
```

```yaml
metadata:
  name: sample-microservice
spec:
  replicas: 3
  selector:
    matchLabels:
      app: sample-microservice
  template:
    metadata:
      labels:
        app: sample-microservice
    spec:
      containers:
      - name: sample-microservice
        image: your-registry/sample-microservice:latest
        ports:
        - containerPort: 8080
```

```

## 4. GraphQL for Microservices APIs:

- GraphQL simplifies microservices communication by providing a single endpoint for querying and mutating data.
- Microservices expose GraphQL APIs, allowing clients to request only the data they need.

**Example (Apollo Server with GraphQL):**

- Define GraphQL schema and resolvers for aggregating data from multiple microservices.

```javascript

const { ApolloServer, gql } = require('apollo-server-lambda');

const typeDefs = gql`

  type Query {

    getUser(id: ID!): User

  }

  type User {

    id: ID!

    name: String!

```
    email: String!
`;

const resolvers = {
  Query: {
    getUser: async (_, { id }) => {
      // Fetch user data from microservices
      return { id, name: 'John Doe', email: 'john@example.com' };
    };

const server = new ApolloServer({ typeDefs, resolvers });

exports.handler = server.createHandler();
```

5. Infrastructure as Code (IaC):

- Infrastructure as Code enables the provisioning and configuration of microservices infrastructure using code.
- Tools like Terraform and AWS CloudFormation automate the deployment of microservices architecture.

Example (AWS CloudFormation):

- Define CloudFormation templates for provisioning AWS resources required by microservices.

```yaml
Resources:
  SampleLambdaFunction:
    Type: 'AWS::Lambda::Function'
    Properties:
      Code:
        S3Bucket: your-bucket
        S3Key: your-function.zip
      Handler: index.handler
      Role: your-role
      Runtime: nodejs14.x
```

6. Observability and Monitoring:

- Observability tools provide insights into the behavior and performance of microservices, facilitating debugging and optimization.

- Metrics, logs, and traces enable monitoring of microservices health and performance.

Example (AWS X-Ray):

- Instrument microservices with X-Ray SDK to trace requests and capture performance metrics.

```javascript
const AWSXRay = require('aws-xray-sdk-core');

const AWS = AWSXRay.captureAWS(require('aws-sdk'));

const lambda = new AWS.Lambda();

exports.handler = async (event) => {

  // Business logic

  AWSXRay.captureFunc('custom-operation', () => {

    // Custom operation

  });
```

7. Hybrid Cloud and Multi-Cloud Deployments:

- Hybrid cloud and multi-cloud strategies allow deploying microservices across different cloud providers or on-premises environments.

- Kubernetes-based solutions like Anthos and OpenShift provide consistency and portability for hybrid cloud deployments.

Example (Google Anthos):

- Deploy microservices to Anthos clusters running on-premises and in Google Cloud.

8. AI/ML Integration with Microservices:

- Integrating AI/ML capabilities into microservices enables intelligent decision-making and automation.
- Serverless machine learning frameworks like TensorFlow Serving and SageMaker facilitate model inference in microservices.

Example (TensorFlow Serving):

- Serve machine learning models as microservices using TensorFlow Serving with Kubernetes.

9. Edge Computing and Edge Microservices:

- Edge computing brings microservices closer to end-users, reducing latency and improving performance.
- Edge microservices run at the network edge, processing data and executing logic closer to where it's generated.

Example (AWS Lambda@Edge):

- Deploy microservices as Lambda functions to CloudFront edge locations for processing requests closer to users.

10. Serverless DevOps and CI/CD Pipelines:

- Serverless DevOps practices emphasize automation, collaboration, and continuous delivery for microservices.
- CI/CD pipelines tailored for microservices workflows enable automated testing, deployment, and monitoring.

Example (GitHub Actions with AWS CodeDeploy):

- Define GitHub Actions workflows for building, testing, and deploying microservices to AWS Lambda.

The future of microservices architecture is characterized by continuous innovation and flexibility, driven by advancements in serverless technologies, containerization, and cloud-native practices. By embracing these trends and leveraging the appropriate tools and patterns, developers can build scalable, resilient, and adaptable microservices architectures to meet the evolving needs of modern applications.

Conclusion

Recap: Your Journey to Building Agile, Scalable Applications

Throughout your journey to building agile, scalable applications, you've embraced the power of serverless microservices architecture. This approach has enabled you to develop applications that are flexible, resilient, and cost-effective, meeting the demands of modern software development. Let's recap the key milestones and insights gained along the way:

1. Embracing Serverless Computing: You started by embracing serverless computing, which abstracts away infrastructure management, allowing you to focus on writing code. This shift in mindset enabled rapid development and deployment of microservices.

2. Designing for Microservices: You adopted microservices architecture, breaking down monolithic applications into smaller, independent services. Each microservice was designed to handle a specific business function or domain, promoting agility and scalability.

3. Leveraging Event-Driven Architecture: Event-driven architecture became a cornerstone of your design approach, enabling loosely-coupled communication between microservices. Events allowed for asynchronous processing, fault tolerance, and scalability.

4. Harnessing the Power of Cloud Services: Cloud services, provided by major cloud providers like AWS, Azure, and Google Cloud, became integral to your architecture. Services such as AWS Lambda, Azure Functions, and Google Cloud Functions allowed you to build and deploy serverless microservices with ease.

5. Implementing Infrastructure as Code (IaC): Infrastructure as Code (IaC) simplified the provisioning and management of cloud resources. Tools like AWS CloudFormation and Terraform enabled you to define your infrastructure in code, ensuring consistency and repeatability across environments.

6. Emphasizing Observability and Monitoring: Observability and monitoring became critical aspects of your architecture, providing insights into the performance and behavior of microservices. Tools like AWS X-Ray, Google Stackdriver, and Prometheus helped you detect and diagnose issues quickly.

7. Automating CI/CD Pipelines: Continuous Integration and Continuous Deployment (CI/CD) pipelines were implemented to automate testing, deployment, and monitoring processes. This automation reduced manual overhead and accelerated the delivery of features and updates.

8. Integrating Machine Learning and AI: You explored integrating machine learning and AI capabilities into your applications, leveraging serverless machine learning frameworks like TensorFlow Serving and Amazon SageMaker. This integration enabled intelligent decision-making and automation within your microservices.

9. Scaling with Kubernetes and Containers: As your applications grew in complexity, you leveraged Kubernetes and containers to manage and orchestrate your microservices at scale. Kubernetes provided features such as service discovery, scaling, and rolling updates, ensuring high availability and reliability.

10. Embracing Edge Computing: To reduce latency and improve performance, you embraced edge computing by deploying microservices closer to end-users. Technologies like AWS Lambda@Edge and Cloudflare Workers enabled you to process requests at the edge, enhancing user experience.

Final Thoughts: The Power of Serverless Microservices Architecture for the Future

As you reflect on your journey, it's clear that serverless microservices architecture holds immense potential for the future of application development. This approach offers unparalleled agility, scalability, and cost-efficiency, enabling developers to build and deploy applications with speed and confidence.

By embracing serverless computing, designing for microservices, and leveraging cloud-native technologies, you've unlocked new possibilities for innovation and growth. The flexibility of serverless microservices architecture allows you to adapt to changing requirements and scale seamlessly as your applications evolve.

As you look ahead, continue to explore emerging trends and advancements in serverless technologies, such as event-driven architectures, machine learning integration, and edge computing. By staying at the forefront of innovation and continuously refining your approach, you'll be well-positioned to build agile, scalable applications that drive success in the digital era.

Appendix

Glossary of Key Terms

Glossary of Key Terms in Microservices Design Patterns for Serverless Applications

1. Microservices Architecture: A software architecture pattern where complex applications are composed of small, independently deployable services, each responsible for a specific business function. Microservices promote modularity, scalability, and agility.

2. Serverless Computing: A cloud computing model where cloud providers dynamically manage the allocation of machine resources, allowing developers to focus on writing code without worrying about infrastructure provisioning or maintenance. Serverless platforms execute code in response to events and automatically scale based on demand.

3. Event-Driven Architecture (EDA): An architectural pattern where components communicate asynchronously via events. In microservices, EDA facilitates loose coupling between services, enabling scalability, fault tolerance, and decoupled interactions.

4. Infrastructure as Code (IaC): The practice of defining and managing infrastructure resources using code, such as YAML or JSON templates. IaC automates the provisioning and configuration of infrastructure, ensuring consistency and repeatability across environments.

5. Continuous Integration/Continuous Deployment (CI/CD): A software development practice where code changes are automatically built, tested, and deployed to production environments. CI/CD pipelines automate the software delivery process, reducing manual overhead and enabling rapid iteration.

6. Observability: The ability to understand the internal state of a system based on external outputs. In microservices, observability encompasses metrics, logs, and traces, providing insights into the performance, health, and behavior of services.

7. Containerization: The process of packaging and deploying applications and their dependencies into lightweight, portable containers. Containers provide isolation and consistency across different environments, making it easier to deploy and manage microservices.

8. Kubernetes: An open-source container orchestration platform for automating the deployment, scaling, and management of containerized applications. Kubernetes provides features such as service discovery, load balancing, and self-healing, making it ideal for running microservices at scale.

9. GraphQL: A query language and runtime for APIs that enables clients to request only the data they need. In microservices, GraphQL serves as a unified interface for aggregating data from multiple services, reducing over-fetching and under-fetching of data.

10. Edge Computing: A distributed computing paradigm where computation is performed closer to the data source or end-user, typically at the network edge. Edge computing reduces latency and bandwidth usage, making it suitable for microservices that require real-time processing and low-latency responses.

11. Machine Learning Integration: The incorporation of machine learning models and algorithms into microservices to enable intelligent decision-making and automation. Serverless machine learning frameworks like TensorFlow Serving and Amazon SageMaker facilitate model inference within microservices.

12. Hybrid Cloud Deployments: A deployment model that combines on-premises infrastructure with public cloud services. In microservices, hybrid cloud deployments offer flexibility and scalability, allowing services to run in multiple environments while maintaining consistency and interoperability.

13. Circuit Breaker Pattern: A design pattern used to prevent cascading failures in distributed systems. In microservices, the circuit breaker pattern temporarily halts requests to a failing service and redirects them to an alternative or cached response, improving system resilience and fault tolerance.

14. Retry Mechanism: A mechanism for automatically retrying failed requests or operations. In microservices, retry logic with exponential backoff is commonly used to handle transient failures and improve reliability.

15. Distributed Tracing: The practice of tracking and logging the execution path of requests as they traverse through distributed systems. Distributed tracing tools like AWS X-Ray and Zipkin enable developers to visualize and debug the flow of requests across microservices.

These key terms provide a foundational understanding of microservices design patterns for serverless applications, empowering developers to design, build, and deploy scalable and resilient architectures in the cloud.

www.ingramcontent.com/pod-product-compliance
Lightning Source LLC
Chambersburg PA
CBHW031607210526
45464CB00004B/1458